James W. (James William) Steele

The Sons of the Border

Sketches of the Life and People of the Far Frontier

James W. (James William) Steele

The Sons of the Border

Sketches of the Life and People of the Far Frontier

ISBN/EAN: 9783337010546

Printed in Europe, USA, Canada, Australia, Japan

Cover: Foto ©ninafisch / pixelio.de

More available books at **www.hansebooks.com**

THE
SONS OF THE BORDER.

SKETCHES OF THE

LIFE AND PEOPLE

OF THE FAR FRONTIER.

BY

JAMES W. STEELE.
("DEANE MONAHAN.")

TOPEKA, KANSAS:
COMMONWEALTH PRINTING COMPANY.
1873.

CONTENTS.

	PAGE.
Introduction	5
The Sons of the Border	9
Chuck	20
New Mexican Common Life	35
The Scout's Mistake	50
Copper-Distilled	66
Jack's Divorce	79
A Harvest-Day with the Pueblos	90
Brown's Revenge	103
A Day with the Padres	122
Joe's Pocket	136
Woman under Difficulties	168
The Reunion of the Ghosts	179
Coyotes	188
The Priest of El Paso	197
La Senorita	212
Peg	222
Captain Jinks	237
Jornada del Muerto	246

INTRODUCTION.

Descriptive literature is nothing unless sectional. True genius is cosmopolitan in its scope, to be sure, and good and grand things in song and story gradually become common property. But the man who attempts to paint humanity in generalities, to picture the universe in its entirety, wastes time and strength in chasing a phantom. Wealth of mind is for all the world, but the digging and coining must be done by patient and careful toil in particular localities. The successful worker in poesy or romance wins his triumphs by concentrating his efforts upon a special set of surroundings in scenery, traditions, thought and manners, and revealing and reflecting the distinguishing features of a given section and the peculiar characteristics of a certain class or division of people through skilful delineations of really striking points. And the striking points of a country or a people are not always the things which stand out most prominently, and first arrest the attention of the casual looker. The grunt of a hog is often worth more than a whole lecture on geology; and a single crisp sentence of slang frequently contains more of actual significance than is embodied in pages of the most accurate and elaborate statistics. The little things are the true indices, as all the great masters have demonstrated; and the little things are caught and fixed only by steady and searching study within fixed limits. Homer, Shakespeare, Scott and Goethe wrote for all mankind; but their universal recognition was gained by the fidelity with which they presented the truly forcible and suggestive peculiarities of their own times, countries and peoples. The same is true of Thackeray and Dickens. And a similar loyalty to local influences in our own land has clothed Sleepy Hollow with immortality and made American literature radiant for all time with the matchless light of the "Scarlet Letter."

The volume to which this is an introduction is noticeably faithful to the theory of which we have spoken, with this qualification: that it relates to people solely—resources, prospects, geography and natural history being but lightly touched upon in the vivid and penetrating portrayals of those far more interesting and suggestive features, men and women. The people delineated are not the denizens of far-off polar or tropic regions, but are intimately connected with us and our interests, in language, religion and common government, if not in race and color. They are, in fact, of our own kind, transformed by the wonderful education of the Border into people of the existence of whom all of us know, but with whose characteristics we have but slight acquaintance. The frontier character, representing the most interesting and fleeting phase of American life,— a life unique in itself and utterly unknown elsewhere under the sun,—has long needed a capable delineator. But men sufficiently gifted with the dramatic faculty, the keen insight into motive and character, the rare power of looking through the crudeness and coarseness of mere outside life and down into the governing ideas and feelings,—the rude sense of honor, the love and hate, the pride and shame, the pathetic and poetic emotions which exist here as everywhere,—have apparently visited the Border but rarely, and made only meagre record of their sights and experiences. At last, however, we have in these pages, in a fair degree of completeness, a true picture of these singular people. There is an indescribable test—a sort of instinct, it may be called—by which truthfulness of description is readily recognized wherever found, no matter how little knowledge the reader may have of the facts. The sketches in this volume seem to us to bear that test. No man could manufacture such characters; no man could tell what is here set down without previous actual study from life. And herein lies the real and enduring value of the volume. It is written to entertain and amuse, it is true; but it is also an accurate record of a fast-fading life which cannot much longer endure, but which makes an important chapter in the social and moral annals of our country.

No one needs to be told, we apprehend, that we but poorly know a man until we get into his heart and study his sensibilities. Human nature is substantially the same under all skies and all circumstances; but the common kinship finds expression in as many different forms as there are variations of climate, culture and experience in the world. To reach the secret springs and exhibit their workings is the only way to portray the individual truthfully and with force and interest. The author of these papers has evidently learned this; and hence one-half of them are stories —romances with but little, if any, foundation in circumstantial fact, and yet just as true to life as if painted from actual occurrences. The real purpose of fiction, so often ignored or misunderstood, has here one of its best illustrations. The story of the Border would be but half told without these imaginary episodes, which deal directly with the deepest thoughts and feelings,—unveiling the very souls of these strange people, so to speak, and letting us look in upon that which they so well knew how to conceal, and yet without a glimpse of which we can but partially understand and imperfectly judge them.

The author has not alone studied the men. It must be stated to his credit that he is the first who has attempted to describe the woman of the Border,—the wife, mother and maiden,—not as she ministers to the baseness of man, but as she is in the home which is as much to her as ours is to us. Of the saloon-girl, the confirmed harlot, and the paramour of the gambler and bandit, we have had enough. It is well that we finally have at least one chapter which does justice to the true woman of the Border, as in isolation and loneliness she bears her burden of toil, privation and suffering.

Scattered throughout these papers, the reader will find many thoughts which he will naturally surmise could only have come from recollections of military life, expressing as they do that peculiar love of arms, the country and the flag which is born of the dangers and delights of soldiership. It was as an officer in the regular army of the United States that the author gained that insight into frontier life and character which he has used so admirably in his sketches. But always silent with regard to his personal experiences, and modestly backward about claiming credit for himself in any respect, no one dreamed, after he returned to private life in 1870, that he possessed so many valuable facts and so many rare impressions as go to make up these chapters, much less the ability to write them with that consummate skill, taste and force which he has displayed. From some personal knowledge of the man,—or boy, as he was and is yet generally considered to be,—and with a vague suspicion that he might be "developed" in a literary way, we solicited him, in December, 1870, to contribute to the pages of the " Kansas Magazine," then about to be started, and with which we were to have the honor of being identified as editor during the first year of its existence—if, fortunately, it 'should survive so long as that. He promptly consented to try the experiment of writing a sketch or story for each of twelve numbers of the periodical, if they proved to have "anything in them." He went his ways, engaged entirely in business pursuits, and every month furnished us a sketch or story, and frequently both. The first was "Jack's Divorce," which appeared in the initial number of the Magazine, and which surprised and delighted us with its originality of interest and strength. Next came "Life Among the New Mexicans," the first real sketch from personal observations ever written of that peculiar population. And this, in turn, was followed by

"Jornada del Muerto," the most graceful and forcible of all his stories, we think. With this, general attention was attracted, and our young friend's writings soon became the special feature of the "Kansas," and the favorite selections of the newspapers all over the country, although prepared from first to last only in the intervals of occasional release from ordinary business thoughts and labors. There could scarcely be a greater mistake than to suppose that these papers were written as a business, or that the time employed in their production was a continuous year. Many of them were written in our presence and sent to the composing-room piecemeal, in appeasement of the traditional imp's cry for "copy," without an attempt at a revision. That they have faults, we are prepared to admit; but that their excellences make full amends for all shortcomings, few will venture to deny.

The collection and publication of the papers in their present form was at our suggestion; and thus arises a god-fatherly relation on our part to a volume with which we are glad to claim a kind of paternal connection. The book, it seems to us, is a timely and valuable addition to our Western literature. The Border and its inhabitants have been too long described and interpreted only through the dime-novel; and it is to their advantage, as well as a matter of general benefit, that they have, even at this late day, been seen, studied and portrayed by a man who has discerned and revealed their real characteristics, and whose writings must for a long time, if not for all time, remain our clearest and truest delineation of that swiftly-disappearing phase of American life which is at once a memory and a prophecy.

HENRY KING.

TOPEKA, DECEMBER 10th, 1872.

THE SONS OF THE BORDER.

NO one would ever learn from the prolific volumes of Abbott, Greeley and the rest, that our country ever developed anything personally characteristic save abstract greatness. Of course not, say the book-makers; America is yet too young to have developed classes whose strangeness sets them apart from the great mass of their countrymen. There is where there is a mistake.

There is a life where habits, prejudices and tastes which have been bred in the bone are forgotten; where the grooves of life are turned awry and broken; and in whose strongly defined, yet fleeting characteristics are to be seen the most remarkable of all the changes which peculiar surroundings are capable of working upon preeducated character.

The Borderer is a man not born, but, unconsciously to himself, *made* by his surroundings and necessities. He may have been born on the Chesapeake or the banks of the Juniata; he may hail from Lincolnshire or Cork: far Western life will clothe him with a new individuality, make him forget the tastes and habits of early life, and transform him into one of that restless horde of cosmopolites who form the crest of the slow wave of humanity which year by year creeps toward the setting sun.

The life of the Border is a transitory one, and fast passing away. The peculiarities which belong to life and men there, when gone in fast advancing civilization, will leave no record of themselves, even as the backwoodsman has left none. The frontier has a language, a religion and a social status of its own. It has a habit of thought and action unique, vigorous and not wanting in the elements which everywhere express religion, honor and pathos. The people whose tastes or whose fates lead them here, have a world to themselves alone. A world of loneliness and lost comforts, where cities, banks, railroads, theatres, churches and scandal have not yet come; a world where births and weddings are few, funeral ceremonies are short, and tears are nearly unknown. It is a land where there is so close an affinity between nature and man that nature is an hourly teacher; a land that is solemn as the sea, and where, as upon the sea, the far blue mists of the horizon bound the world. The days, unchanged by the ceremonies and observances of civilization, are all alike, each one as melancholy as a Puritan Sabbath. Nature is herself, and spreads her feasts and acts her caprices for her own pleasure. Acres of flowers, leagues of beauty, bloom and fade and come again, unseen by man. Solitary birds fly lazily by. The animals stare at the new animal—the passing man—almost unscared, and silence is a power.

And yet, the Borderer is not a child of nature. Men never are. That term is a license of the poets. He is a creature of education; but an education so peculiar that the term scarcely expresses it. He is a very different character from the backwoodsman who has been called his prototype, and in all respects is a much more modern creation. He who a generation ago was engaged in felling the forests of Ohio and Indiana, was clad in buckskin and moccasons, and practised in a homely manner the virtues of hospitality, uncouth but disinterested kindness and general honesty. If he was ignorant of the graces of civilization, he also knew of few of the vices. He had not been in cities, and carried their sins with him into the wilderness. The weapon of his day was an honest rifle, and not an arsenal of death slung about the waist. In all these things the modern frontiersman sets at nought the idealisms of Cooper, the time-honored traditions of the Wabash, and the well-established ideas of novel-reading mankind.

The ideal Borderer, the type of his class from Western Kansas to the Rio Grande, you will find clad in calfskin boots, with broad-rimmed hat worn askew, and his nether limbs encased in fancy cassimeres. There are rings upon his fingers, and blazing jewels upon his breast. He is loud and defiant in dress, manners and general deportment. He clings with the tenacity of second nature to the language of the dance-house and the brothel. The happy thought of Colonel Colt, which has filled more unmarked graves than the plague, and eternally settled more disputes than all juries, is his constant and valued companion, and he wears his rakish hat awry upon his oily locks with the air of the king of all the loafers.

But he is not a loafer. He is quarrelsome, jealous in honor, and still very much of a man and a friend to those who understand him. He makes no reservation of actual impressions and thoughts, but in this he is only unnecessarily sincere and independent. He will take a stranger's last dollar at a game which he does not understand, but he will likewise lend and share to the last cent and the last morsel. He hates "airs," cannot abide to be patronized, and is ugly to all who chance to disagree with him. His great fault is that he is intolerant, but he is brave, sincere and faithful when once enlisted in any cause.

This kind of man, with the many variations which exist among classes always, *is* the frontiersmen. California has known him these twenty years. He is here and there in all the villages in Colorado and New Mexico, and his habitation is in every sheltered nook upon the great Plains. With all his faults it may justly be said of him that he is a man who depends upon his courage, who has chosen his life and will never leave it, and who is the fit and capable vidette who stands upon the verge of the mighty civilization which is destined to follow him, when he and his unconscious work shall have passed away.

It is not necessarily a startling announcement that the Borderer does not feel called upon to live entirely without the comfort and solace of woman. Men may be saddened, but not astonished, to know that the bold-faced curse of the by-streets of the most populous and enlightened cities of the world is also here, bolder, gaudier and more shameless than ever. Ministering to every baseness, inciting to every crime, worse than her associates by so much as woman fallen is always worse than man, the drunken queen of the *demi monde* flaunts her finery among the shanties of every frontier town.

But there is another class, who, in a feminine way, are like unto their husbands and brothers. They are indeed few, and it will be long before there is a surplus of maiden ladies upon the frontier. How or why any of them ever came there is something of a mystery. But they live in the ranche and the adobe, and are wives and mothers, and are content, and it is hardly superlative to say, as happy as their more elegant sisters of the East. Their nearest neighbor may be twenty miles away, their chances for gossip few and far between, and all their amusements and occupations homely and man-like. They know more of the economy of the corral, the qualities of horses and the habits of the coyote, than they do of the prevailing fashions, and the cunning variations in length of trail and size of *chignon*. But the neat bed in the corner, the clean hearth, the drapery of the one poor window, and the trailing-vine over the low roof, in many a lonely frontier house, proclaim the touch, the taste, the love and care with which in loneliness and poverty and isolation, a woman still adorns the spot which is her home.

There are children, too. You need not think to escape the cry of infancy by immigrating westward. They never heard a school-house bell, and are ignorant of the functions of a Sunday-school superintendent. They are even deprived of the ordinary amusements of children. They ride no gates, slide upon no cellar-doors, and make no small escapades, to be found and carried home by the police. But the mud-pie proprietorship of a hundred leagues is thiers. All their lives they have heard the bark of the coyote, and watched for the coming and going of the bison, and are in the majority of instances the tow-headed, boggle-eyed urchins which English children the world over are apt to be.

Partly from circumstances attending traffic, particularly freighting, but mainly from what may be called the migratory instinct, most of the people of the far frontier owe the fact of their residence there. So far east as Western Kansas, there is still a more natural motive— the desire of obtaining a home and land. There is no more natural illustration than is here apparent, of how the human mind goes back in its desires to the original source of all wealth, and to the original meaning of the word *home*,—a home which is ours, because we have made it. In the search for this, there is no danger which can daunt, no difficulty which can discourage. The pertinacity with which the pre-emptors and squatters have clung to their poor homes, amid surroundings in which there seems so little present happiness and so little future hope, is not the least surprising feature of their hard life. But with regard to the class with which this article has mainly to do, the question as to why they are there, and what they find to do, is harder to answer. The Plains ranche proper is always a small store, in which is sold bacon, flour and a villanously poor article of whiskey. The travel is mainly confined to certain roads, and, notwithstanding the trans-continental lines of railroad, is at certain seasons of the year by no means inconsiderable. By this travel, the ranchero lives. The brown walls of his hovel, seen from afar, are hailed with delight by men who have not drunk or smoked since the night at the last stopping-place. To pass without drinking, would be to the average Plainsman an act of folly little short of absolute idiocy.

But the proportion of people who live on the Border without any visible means of support is larger than anywhere else outside of metropolitan cities. The hangers-on of the ranches go and come unquestioned. Their sinister, bearded faces disappear, and they are gone, perhaps only for an hour, though if forever it leads to no inquiry and excites no alarm. The Anglo-Saxon can become anything. He can be Indianized and Mexicanized as easily as not, and upon the frontier he becomes an Arab. Not a weak imitation or an intentioned pattern, but of his own kind, and after his own fancies and necessities. Taciturn, suspicious and courageous,—hospitable in peace and desperate and unscrupulous in enmity,—the Bedouin of the Border, organized and armed, would make the most efficient *corps* ever formed for partisan warfare.

The Border is a field for the gathering together of all kinds and races. Here is the patient, plodding, phlegmatic German, fast forgetting every tradition of his fatherland in the absorbing wildness which makes all men alike. Here is the Irishman, with the rich brogue of Tipperary still upon his tongue, but changed in all else which speaks of the green isle of peat, potatoes and blarney. And here is the down-east Yankee, forgetful of all the ideas of the land of Puritans and hard-cider, turning all his native cunning and shrewdness into account at poker and California-Jack. Here is the broad-shouldered son of the South, still speaking the mincing dialect which is borrowed in the name of gentility from the thick tongue of the negro, but for a wonder forgetting to insert "Sir" at the beginning, middle and ending of every sentence. But all are changed, at least in name. The German has become "Dutch Bill," or "Sam" or "Jake;" the Irishman is "Pat" or "Paddy," adding any further pseudonym which may designate that particular Irishman. The New Englander glories in the name of "Yank," and the Southerner answers with great alacrity to the name of "Tennessee" or "Kaintuck," and sometimes to "Pike" or "Cracker." Thus is rampant democracy made manifest. The real names of individuals are utterly unknown to companions who have known them for years. Any peculiarity of person or history produces its apt cognomen of recognition. The man who squints is "Cockeye" for all time. The lame man is "Limpey," and the tall man "Slim Dick." The surprising feature of this frontier fashion is that these names are accepted and gloried in. Indeed, those which are born of some peculiarity of history are proudly borne. To be "Buffalo Bill" or "Fighting Bob" is to be famous.

"Mister" is the designation of a stranger, but if a Borderer calls an individual "mister" after he has known him a week, he means some fine morning to kill him unless he changes his opinion of his merits.

Brusk and rude as all this seems, there is no land where the established forms are more rigidly exacting. "Take suthin'?" means mortal offence and an ever-remembered grudge if the invited man refuse. If you are asked to "set up an' eat," it is not a mere form, but you are not only really welcome, but expected to return the neighborly compliment when your host comes your way. In this immense scope of country, men who live two hundred miles apart are often near neighbors and intimate friends. The necessities of the frontier produce a Freemasonry in comparason with which the actual brotherhood is a tame and meaningless thing. If a ranchman lend his neighbor a mule and tell him to leave it at Sim's or Slocum's, a hundred miles away, he is certain of finding the animal there when wanted. Honesty and punctuality are the current exchange of the country, and a short shrift and sudden end is the meed of absolute necessity to him who wrongs his neighbor.

Another band of union among all white men, is common enmity to the universal enemy, the Indian. Hatred of the Apache and the Kiowa will be the uppermost feeling in the Borderer's mind as long as there is a disputed territory, claimed alike by him and his enemy. Year by year the ranks of the warriors are thinned in many an encounter which is never heard of in the world of newspapers, and year by year the frontiersman counts fresh accessions to his ranks. While right and justice and policy are discussed, the contest proceeds without any abatement between the parties interested. The sentence of doom which is written against the red man is utterly irrevocable. The horde who invade his hunting grounds, are hardy, adventurous, bold and as cunning as he. Within a century one of the great divisions of a common family will have curiously passed away, and his only history will be the history of his decadence and death, preserved in the scanty annals of his first and last enemy, the Borderer.

But there is still another side to the frontiersman's friendship. His neighborly courtesies are all outside of the obligations imposed by the sixth commandment. The revolver is not eternally carried about for nothing, and its owner is quick of hand and eye, and generally sure of his weopon and his aim. There is no man upon whom a reckless code of honor is so fatally and foolishly binding. An insult, fancied or real, is settled then and there with a life, and the bystanders are the judges of the fairness of the transaction. To maul and gouge is childish, to murder is gentlemanly and proper, and withal the fashion. The old code of the duello was a tame and insipid thing compared with a row in a saloon in a border town. There is no code, no law, no jury. Each man, in the heat of passion, is the judge of the effect of the foolish word, the drunken insult, or the hastily-spoken taunt, and therefore gives his own life or takes another for it, as depends upon his soberness, his quickness or his courage. Talk of the fashions which rule society! Tell of hoops, and *chignons*, and bustles, and Dolly Vardens! On the Border, men willingly die to be in the fashion.

Men become accustomed to all surroundings except prison-walls, and to solitude easiest of all. The frontiersman would smile if you told him his life was a monotonous one. But wanting even the newspaper, he is even more gregarious than other men, and a companion of some kind, brute in the want of something human, is necessary to existence. The dog, dear as he is to many men everywhere, is doubly a friend in the wilderness. His lonesome master sleeps and eats and talks with him. He may be the mangiest cur that ever barked. No matter: it is not a country in which to be particular. There is another animal, which commonly leads a persecuted life and dies a violent death among Christian people, which here would find long life and due appreciation. What would not the frontiersman give for a cat? The most comical comforter of loneliness I ever knew was a donkey—a small specimen which could be carried in one's arms. As this long-eared, solemn-countenanced little ass stalked about the shanty, investigated the cookery, and even climbed upon the bed, its jolly master would sit and hold his sides with mirth. But the apportunity for companionship with his own kind, never passes unused. There are nightly gatherings at every ranche, and the resource for amusement is usually the art which is as old as Babel; the art of story-telling. Each man tells of his own adventures, palming them off for very truth, and, as every listener knows, making them as he goes out of whole cloth. Some of the most outrageous travesties upon truth ever said or sung have beguiled the dull hours in the frontier cabin. The next resource is the card-table, and in mining districts the sums which change hands in a night would startle the *habitues* of Saratoga or Baden-Baden. With nearly all frontiersmen gambling is a passion, and some of them are the most thoroughly accomplished members of the card-dealing fraternity.

The man who shall transfer to canvas some one of the

scenes which each midnight brings to the inner room of the trader's store in a New Mexican mining-camp, and shall do it well, will preserve for all time the most striking feature of American frontier life. We shall see the dead silence and rapt attention as the guttering candles flare upon each sun-browned and grizzled face, the hard hands and hairy arms, and the look of covert exultation as the winner draws towards him the coin and bags of yellow dust. We shall read the quick glance which suspects a cheat, and the deep curse which records a mistake. And standing there, almost as intent as the players, are they who watch the fascinating passion in in its varying record of gain and loss. The dim light will throw the rough beams into grim indistinctness, and lurk in grotesque shadows in corners. But permeating all—the essence of the picture—will be that ghastly suggestion of folly and ruin which mere words can not paint; that look in faces which tells of the sacrifice and homelessness and toil of years gone in a night, and also of that bewitching hope which waits ever upon the devotees of the god of chance, the end of which is despair, broken hearts and death.

CHUCK.

IF you stand upon a certain bluff on the south side of the Arkansas River a few miles above the mouth of the Purgatoire, in the dawn of morning, you will be the spectator of a scene not easily forgotten in future wanderings. Eastward stretches dimly away the winding, sedgy valley of the dreariest river of the west,— treeless, sandy, desolate. All around you are the endless undulations of the wilderness. Beneath you are the yet silent camps of those who are here to-day and gone to-morrow. Westward is something you anticipate rather than see: vague and misty forms lying upon the horizon. But while the world is yet dark below and around you, and there is scarce the faintest tinge of gray in the east, if you chance to look northward you will see something crimson high up against the sky. At first it is a roseate glow, shapeless and undefined. Then it becomes a cloud-castle, battlemented and inaccessible, draped in mist and hung about with a hovering curtain of changing purple. But as it grows whiter and clearer, the vague outlines of a mighty shape appear below it, stretching downward toward the earth. What you see is the lofty pinnacle which has gleamed first in the flying darkness, sun-kissed and glorified in the rosy mornings of all the centuries. It is Pike's Peak, ninety miles away.

Perchance before you turn to leave the spot you may mechanically glance at your immediate surroundings. If you do, you will have before you at once the two great types of changelessness and frailty; for at your feet, scarce noticed in its lonely humility, is a single low mound, turfless and yellow, unadorned by even so much as a cross or an inscription, but telling, nevertheless, that old story in which no man needs an interpreter: that here rests another of the wanderers, and that there is no land so lonely that it has not its graves.

There may be a story more or less interesting, connected with every one of the unnumbered graves of the Plains. The rough lives that end here have all a history. But no one remembers it. Here, as in busy streets, the lives which once ended are deemed worthy of remembrance, are few and far between. But this lone and wind-kissed mound upon the hill-top, albeit unmarked and seldom seen, has about it an interest not common to the rest, for it is the grave of a woman.

Years ago, a victim of the nomadic instinct named Lemuel Sims, a man who had forsaken his home in the Missouri bottoms for a gold-hunting journey to California, and who, after many changes, had again started eastward, was finally stranded upon the banks of the Arkansas, within the magic circle of protection around old Fort Lyon. Sims had grown middle-aged in wandering, and had consumed almost the last remains of that dogged energy in migration which is the characteristic of his class, by the time he reached a spot than which it would have been hard to find one more utterly wanting in attractions. But he was not alone, for he had a wife who had been his companion in all his journeys, and three daughters, who had irregularly come in upon his vicissitudes. In sending those guests which are often unwelcome but never turned away, the old man's fates had not been kind. What he needed was boys,—boys of whom hereafter should be made the ranchers, the Indian fighters, the hunters and the poker-players who should diligently follow in the footsteps of their wild predecessors, and live hard and die suddenly.

When Sims came to his last residence, the order of march was as follows: First, Sims, a hundred yards in advance, gun in hand; secondly, two mules and an old wagon, Mrs. Sims at the helm; thirdly, three cows, four sheep, four dogs; and behind all, two freckled, brawny moccasoned girls. The third and youngest, the darling of the family,—too young, indeed, for service,—occupied a cosy nest among the household goods, and peeped out from beneath the tattered cover, plump, saucy, and childishly content. She had acquired the name of Chuck, abbreviated from *chicquita*,—" little one,"—and amid all the changes which befell her thereafter, the name clung to her as part of herself.

The Sims "outfit" was only an integral portion of a cavalcade of such, strong enough for all purposes of society and defence. Months had passed since the family began this last move. The long summer days had passed, and the nipping nights and scanty pasturage were the cause of the premature ending of the journey. Having stopped only for a night, they had concluded to stay until spring, or some other time when a spasm of the migratory disease should seize them. But the rough house of cottonwood logs Sims made with the help of his family, was in a sheltered nook which soon became home-like. There was game in abundance, and what was not immediately consumed the old man exchanged for groceries at the post. What was still more fortunate, Sim's house was near the route of travel, and he could indulge his love of gossip, as well as furnish an occasional meal to travellers. When spring came, the stock had grown fat, and, save the mules, had increased in numbers a hundred fold. Impelled by the force of circumstances, a small garden was enclosed, and it came about that by June the frontiersman and his family found themselves prospering beyond anything in their past history. The shanty took upon itself the dignity of a ranche; and in truthfulness it is necessary to state that the commodity which met the readiest and most profitable sale was a fluid which, chemically considered, it were slanderous to call whiskey. "Simsis" became known far and wide, and the proprietor began to think himself gaining upon the world, both in money and fame,—two things which, in the unfortunate constitution of society, are not sufficiently distributed. But this new era of prosperity was not due to Sims's management. It grew mainly out of the fact that he had three daughters. The unfortunate constitution of the family was the direct cause of its unwonted thrift. Any white woman in such a place is an enticement not to be resisted by the average Plainsman, and "Sims's gals" were celebrities over an extent of country as large as the State of New York.

But as time passed and the small herds increased, the females became objects of a still profounder interest. They were spoken of as heiresses. Nevertheless, at the pinch, no amount of money could have married either of the two eldest daughters. They were tall, gaunt and coarse. They were as ignorant as Eve, and had performed the duties of masculinity so long that either of them was nearly a match for a cinnamon bear. Not so with the youngest. The most courtly and polished dames in the land have seldom displayed as much in the way of personal endowment as this one rose among the thistles. Fair-skinned and blue-eyed, strong and graceful, petted from infancy and nurtured in comparative ease, healthful in sentiment as in body, she was a special attraction, and came seldom in contact with the rough characters who frequented her father's house. And she had the mind of the family. Her opinions were the law of the house, and she occupied her autocratic position without embarrassment and ruled without check. Old Sims was her man-servant, and her mother was only a privileged associate and adviser. As for her huge sisters, they continually rebelled and always obeyed. There is a mysterious law of primogeniture by which children sometimes embody the characteristics of distant ancestors, and discarding the nearer family traits and circumstances, reproduce the vices and virtues which are long forgotten, and the countenances which have been mouldering for a century. There must have been some rare old blood in the Sims family, for this last scion of a race which had been subjected to all the influences of the frontier,— hardship and toil in the Alleghanies, ague and laziness in the Missouri bottoms, and poverty always,—was totally unlike her family and her surroundings. The sprawling feet, gaunt limbs, great brown hands, coarse complexions and carroty hair of her sisters and mother were things they had apart. Nobody knew or ever asked how Chuck had learned to read, or became possessed of certain well-thumbed books and stray newspapers. No one ever inquired into the mystery of how her garments came to fit her round figure with a neatness which was a miracle to the uninitiated, or why the yellow coils lay so grace-upon her shapely head. Finally, the pervading force which directed all things in and around the ranche came to be almost unquestioned. A beauty with a will is a power: a beauty with brains and a will is the most complete of despots.

The Sims family had been five years in this locality, and mainly through the ability of the youngest child, now a mature woman, aided by the circumstance of a fortunate location, had acquired cattle, money and respectability. The money and the respectability were easily cared for, because Chuck carried them both upon her person; but the herd which was gathered nightly into the corral was the lure of final destruction. The charmed circle of safety which was drawn around the military post was an indefinite and uncertain one, and the incursions of Apaches are governed by no conventionality. After long delay, and frequent smaller thefts, came the final swoop which took all.

Old Sims and Chuck started to go to the post. The presence of the latter was necessary to keep the former from getting drunk and falling into the hands of military minions, to be incarcerated in the guard-house. In the perfect peacefulness and serenity of the early morning, it seemed impossible that danger and death could lie in wait so near. As the old man dug his heels into the flanks of his mule, and Chuck looked complacently back from her seat upon a pony only less wilful than his rider, the two little dreamed that it was the last time they were ever to see "Sims's Ranche."

As they threaded their way along the intricacies of the trail, Chuck of course in the lead, the old man labored diligently to bring out the capacities of of his mule wherever the path was wide enough to permit his riding beside his daughter. In truth he had something to say to her concerning those matters in which girls are always interested and about which they are always unwilling to talk. A confidential conversation with his daughter was one of Sims's ungratified ambitions,—a thing which in late years he had often attempted and as often failed in accomplishing. She cared for him, was kind and loving, but seemed to have no ideas in common with him; and do what he would this morning, he could not keep pace with her. When two persons are thus together there is frequently an unconscious idea of the thoughts of one in the mind of the other, and the girl kept steadily ahead. But the subject was one which weighed upon the old man's mind, and despairing of nearer approach he presently called out from behind:

"Chuck?"

"Well, what is it?" came from the depths of the sun-bonnet in front.

"I want ter know, now, *honest*, what yer goin' to do with them two fellers which air one or t' other of em allus 'round our house lookin' fur you. It looks as though Sairey, bein' the oldest, shud hev some kind of a chance,—and she did afore you growed up,—but I rec'on, *now*, there's no use thinkin' uv that till you 're gone. Now, as atween these fellers, I'd like to know"—and plaintively—"'pears to me like I've a right to know, which uv 'em you're goin' to take. I cudent be long a choosin' ef 't was me. W'y, Tom Harris is big an' hansum, and rides forty mile every week fur to git a sight uv ye. I kin tell frum that feller's looks that he'd swim the Arkansaw and fight anything fur ye."

The face in the sun-bonnet grew red as a pansy at the mention of the name; but the old man did not see that, and he continued:

"But I'm mainly oneasy on account of there bein' two

sich. When Tom an' the slick-lookin' feller from Maxwell's is there at the same time, they passes looks which means everything that two sich fellers can do fur to win. *I* don't like t' other feller; neither does the old woman. He'd do a'most anything, in my opinion, an' if you don't make choice atween 'em soon them fellers 'll fight, and that's *sartin*."

The face, which had been rosy, grew slightly pale as he talked. The old man had told his daughter nothing she did not already know; but she was startled to think that the hatred of the two men had been noticed by another. The question in Chuck's heart was not which of the two men she would take, but how to get rid of the disappointed one. Therefore, woman like, she had encouraged neither of them. To her acute mind the difficulty had been a trouble for weeks, and the words of her father were a fresh cause for disquiet.

Old Sims, having thus broken the ice would have continued, but his daughter stopped him with an exclamation, and pointed to the sand at their feet. Sims approached and peered cautiously at the spot his daughter indicated. There they were, not an hour old, the ugly inturned moccason-tracks of four, eight, a dozen Indians. In a woman, timidity and wit are often companions to each other, and Chuck drew in her horse with a determined air. "I don't like that," said she; "I'm going back. It can do us no harm if the herd is driven home, and I want to see it done;" and she turned her horse.

"W'y now," said Sims, "what's the use? Sich things aint oncommon,—come on."

"You can go alone if you think best," she answered.

Before he could reply she was gone, and irritated by what he considered a useless panic, he doggedly continued his journey toward the post. The sight of an Indian-trail eight miles from home seemed a poor cause for fright, even in a woman, Sims thought as he continued his journey; and it was not that which caused her to retreat; it was to avoid being questioned further upon the topic he had broached. "Cur'us critters is wimmin," he said to himself as he jogged on.

Sims spent that night, unconscious of its horrors, happy drunk in the post guard-house.

An apprehension which she could hardly understand, filled the mind of the girl as she urged her pony toward home. Her father's talk added to her excitement, and she thought of what Tom Harris, strong, daring and handsome, would be at such a time. His tall figure, cheery face and handsome dress, as he sat on his horse at her father's door, blithe and fresh after his ride of forty miles for her sake, came vividly before her. Even in the midst of her anxiety and nervousness she felt that she and Tom, united in purpose and effort, could do anything in this world. Such were the strong woman's thoughts of a man whom she loved because he was even stronger than she.

Two miles from home, and the rider's heart sank at the sight of a column of smoke on the verge of the familiar horizon. Frightened indeed, now, she urged her pony to his utmost, and at the crest of the hill that overlooked the nook in which stood her home, the truth burst upon her that while her father had talked to her of her lovers, and while she was yet speculating upon the foot prints in the sand, the Indian torch was being applied, and now herds, house, mother and sisters were all gone.

Amid all the conflicting griefs and terrors of the moment, arose an overwhelming sense of utter loneliness and helplessness. The beautiful and subtle strength of a woman may guide, but it can neither guard or revenge. There seemed no help, and the girl wished in her heart she had gone with the rest. But she was not so entirely alone, for as she came nearer she saw the tall figure of Tom Harris, newly alighted from an all-night ride, standing by his panting horse, so entirely occupied with a despairing contemplation of the smouldering ruins that he had not as yet noticed her approach. But when he turned and recognized her, his grim face took color like a flash. In truth, Tom's paleness was not the pallor of fear. Words were inadequate to express the tone in which he had cursed the Apaches, by all that was holy and all that was evil, as he stood contemplating the burning house, and thinking with a pang which penetrated his very soul that *she* was among the victims. But when he heard, then turned and saw her, all was thenceforth fair and serene to Tom Harris. With a frontiersman's quick perception of circumstances and situations of this kind, he understood and asked no questions.

"The 'Paches are clear gone with everything, Miss," he said. "They must a' done it in ten minits. Come, git down now, won't ye? That pony's about done for, and— W'y, now, Miss, 't aint no use grievin.' Ye can't bring 'em back, and ye can't catch the Injuns,— not to-day. I'll be even with 'em if I live, but I've knowed a many sich things in my time, and—"

Tom stopped, for he had a sense of how tame and meaningless his rude efforts at comfort were to the silent and horror-stricken woman before him, whose whole soul seemed engrossed in a struggle with the calamity which had befallen her. The well-meaning fellow went some distance apart and waited. And while he waited, the white despairing face grew still whiter, and she slipped helplessly from the pony and lay a limp and lifeless heap upon the ground. This was the time of the frontiersman's utter despair. In all his life's vicissitudes there had been none like this. But all his endeavors were the sensible ones of a practical man. He knew nothing of what he ought to do for the restoration of lost consciousness, and was afraid to try. But with the celerity of habit he stripped the thick blankets from his horse and the pony, and hurriedly spread them in the shade by the bankside. Then he made a pillow of his saddle, and with a blush that rose to his temples, and a thrill which went to his finger-ends, he lifted the girl, and strong as he was, fairly staggering under the burden, laid her upon the couch he had made. He took his own soft serape, with its crimson stripes, and spread it for a covering; filled his canteen and placed it near her; and then sat down afar off and picked holes in the ground with his long knife, and whistled softly, and sighed and groaned within himself. Tom loved the woman who lay there, and because he loved her he was afraid of her. Most men experience the same feeling once in their lives.

But there had been another and an unseen spectator of all this. We can not tell by what peculiar conjunction of the planets things fall out in this world as they do. But while Tom was executing his plans of comfort the "slick-lookin' feller from Maxwell's" was watching afar off. He came no nearer, because he did not at first understand the situation. The burning building suggested Indians, and he wanted no closer acquaintance with them, should they still be there. But while he watched he saw and recognized the two persons, and a pang of jealousy entered his heart. Then he stayed away because he desired to husband for future misrepresentation and use the circumstances to which he had been an unseen witness, and finally rode away, baffled, pondering in his cowardly heart some scheme which could harm his formidable rival.

The afternoon passed slowly away, snd still Tom Harris kept watch. Occasionally he crept on tiptoe and looked at his charge. She seemed asleep. Finally he hobbled the two horses to prevent escape, gathered some of the vegetables in the desolate garden, and stifled a strong man's hunger with young radishes, green tomatoes and oilless lettuce. He could afford to wait, for he was engaged in what he wondered to think was, in the midst of the smoking signs of rapine and captivity, the most delightful task of his life. He did not know that hours ago the occupant of the couch had opened her eyes, and with returning consciousness had touched the crimson-barred serape; had seen the stalwart sentinel sitting afar off, and then had fallen into the deep slumber of grief.

Through the long watches of the night the sleepless frontiersman passed back and forth, listening to the chatter of the coyote and the gray wolf's long-drawn howl. He scared away the stealthy footsteps of the prowlers of the night, and listened and waited. Anon he crept close to the side of the couch and listened for the breathing of the sleeper; then crept away again with the happy consciousness that he and love had all the wilderness to themselves.

In the early morning he heard the clank of sabres and the hum of voices; and a troop of cavalry appeared from the post, and among them Old Sims, red-eyed and trembling, but sobered by apprehension and grief. The man from Maxwell's had told of the raid at the post, and he had reasons of his own for doing so. They left men and means for the conveying of the woman back to the post, and Old Sims returned with her. As for Tom, the soldiers gave him something to eat, and he mounted his horse and accompanied them upon the trail. His step was as light and his heart as merry as though he had slept in his bed, for as he looked back the last time the face he saw was sad and white, but the eyes were the eyes of a woman who looks after one she loves.

Frail of body but strong of purpose, the unconquerable spirit of Old Sims's daughter employed itself in directing the erection of a house upon the spot which had been so long a home. In less than a month she and Sims were again established in the prarie nook, in a cabin not differing materially from the former, but surrounded by a palisade which bade defiance to Indian assault. The couple were not poor, and while the old man drowned the past in half-drunk inanity, the dependents of the house did the work the two daughters had once done. Chuck, stately and sad, but softened, seemed daily to wait and watch for something which never came, and of which she never spoke. The troops with which Tom Harris went away had returned. They told of a day's running fight, which was duly mentioned in general-orders, but in which they had suffered no losses. If Tom had returned to his place, why did he not come again so Sims's Ranch? Chuck said to herself. And then there was his beautiful serape; he might even come for *that*. But he did not. The man from Maxwell's did come; and so placid was his reception that he went away again with bitterness in his heart. He came again. The pale-faced woman had drooped a little, he thought, and cared even less for his distinguished company than before. But even while she cooled his ardor with a grand dignity, she seemed waiting for some one to come in, and listening for some footstep. But lately this man had become the possessor of a secret which filled his heart with exultation. He learned it at the post, where it was mentioned by careless soldiers, ignorant of its fearful import. The loss of a man is nothing, and the few of them who had been lately at Sims's did not even know of the fact. The only circumstance about the affair at all remarkable in the eyes of those sons of Mars was, that a man whose name was hardly known and now not remembered, who went with them only "for fun" and through a peculiar hatred of Apaches, should be the only man to fall. True, he was foremost; was a splendid-looking fellow; and they thought it a pity, and buried him where he fell. Therefore this suitor of Sims's daughter, possessed with the cunning which sometimes defeats itself, bethought him of this chance shot, and deemed that if it did him no good it might at least wound the placidity which he hated. So one day as he stood at the door, smarting under a cool reception and no good-bye at all, he remarked to Sims:

"Seems to me, old man, you and yer darter is waitin' for suthin' that'll never come. She need n't slight *me* a-waitin' fur better company. Tom Harris was killed by the 'Paches which burned yer shanty; an' that's a fact ye kin think uv at yer leisure." And he laughed to himself like a hyena as he went away.

Old Sims staggered into the house where his daughter sat, and dropped into a seat. Even his weak mind had a conception of the fatefulness of the tidings he bore, and he hesitated in the task of disclosure.

"Chuck," he said, "do you 'member that day you found the Injun-trail?"

She started, and nodded assent.

"Do ye 'member my talk about them two lovers o' yourn? Eh? Well, Tom ain't a-comin' any more, 'cause he's—now *I* can't help it darter,—Tom's *dead!*"

She must have known it in her heart before, she changed so slightly at the word. Perhaps she had only hoped against hope, having long ago learned, as she lay on the couch he had made for her through that summer night, that the man whose heart had then been measured in the strength and sleeplessness and honor and courage of a great love, would have returned had he been alive. She only rose and tottered to the bedside, whose topmost cover was a serape; but she never left it again. The one mighty love of a life in whose sordid surroundings it was the one glimpse of something brighter and happier, was as much a reality as though it had been plighted a thousand times. Perhaps the ancestral courage and hope which had come to her through such degenerate veins helped her to die.

That life is complete which has in it only the remembrance of a passion such as this. If we lived a century we should get no more, for the sublimities of life are ever incomplete. The bright, strong face which had looked back at her so hopefully in the saddle-leap, a few weeks ago, was still hers. What wonder that since he could not come to her,—to the house that, with a strong woman's fancy, she had built for him to protect her in,—she should go to his.

NEW MEXICAN COMMON LIFE.

THERE is a country far to the south-west in which everything is crude, new and undeveloped; where the evidences of enterprise and the settlements of white men are few; but which is, notwithstanding, the seat of an ancient and Christian civilization, whose Capital is the oldest town in America but one.

Several centuries have elapsed since the Spanish tongue and the Catholic faith became recognized and accustomed institutions in New Mexico. They antedate the settlement of Jamestown and the romance of Pocahontas. The then mighty Spanish power had founded a government here before the City of New York had passed from the hands of its Dutch founders. The roads and mountain passes which are traveled with such precaution now were the routes of trade long before the first wagon-road had been made across the Alleghanies. While the Delawares and the Hurons were still fighting to hold their ancient possessions on the Eastern coast against the aggressions of the white men, the aborigines of this country had long been converted to Slavery and Christianity; always excepting those tribes whose hands are against every man, and who were then, as they are now, the scourge of civilization. There are churches here in which the disciples of Loyola said mass more than two hundred years ago, and mines whose shafts have been closed almost three centuries.

But interesting as the history of this strange country is, the New Mexico and the New Mexican of to-day are much more so. The very names of the ancient towns whose walls are now grass-grown ridges of earth, have passed away with their inhabitants. Almost the last vestige of the civilization of conquest is gone. All that the Mexican now knows he could easily have learned since the country came under the control of the United States, and in the comparatively short time during which American enterprise has had a foothold. Everywhere, even in places now so wild and so nearly inaccessible that they will be among the last reclaimed, there are dim signs of a curious past, which has gone without monuments and without a history.

The great feature of the country, geographically, is mountains—nothing but mountains. They are not the picturesque and tree-clad hills of the East, but are bold and bare and brown, and piled peak upon peak, with the plateaux lying hidden between, for hundreds of silent and desolate miles. Here and there is a stream, or a marshy spring, and sometimes a cluster of huts in the midst of a few fertile acres. But on every hand the rugged peaks cut a frowning outline against a sky the bluest and fairest in the world. These mountains are, however, the repositories in which lie locked immense and varied supplies of mineral wealth, mostly undeveloped, and probably undiscovered. And they are not without inhabitants, for they are the domain, the inaccessible and chosen home, of the Apache. None but the Apache knows them, and none but he would be able to find sustenance there.

The centres of life and trade in the country are the small towns in the great valley of the Rio Grande, for miles along whose sandy, insect-haunted stream continuous villages extend. There are also settlements which live under the shadow and protection of the military posts.

Places most dangerous and remote are naturally the location of the military, and it is curious to note how soon a small settlement will grow up among the mountains or beside some spring under the auspices of military protection.

It is a land where nature in all her forms seems to delight in coarseness and ruggedness. Every shrub is thorny, and every undeveloped twig has a horny and needle-like point. The flowers are few, and of trees there are none save those which grow sparsely on the banks of the streams. But there is an interminable wilderness of *mezquit*, a thorny and ugly shrub, whose beans furnish a staple article of savage food, whose roots are fuel, and from whose tough branches are made the bows which, in the hands of an Apache, so often send an unexpected and noiseless death to the traveler.

From all there is in geography, and from any discussion of resources and prospects, all of which claim their share of interest for the future, and have already been more or less accurately described, we turn to that which is always a central point of interest in a strange land, the character and habits of its people.

In the question of the original annexation of the immense territory, a part of which included New Mexico, to the United States, there were no more uninterested people than the New Mexicans themselves. They are not of that class who of their own accord long for freedom and sigh for the privilege of self-government. The difference between the rule of a government that for so many years has been alternately an anarchy and a monarchy, and one whose great struggle for life was fought out almost unheard on these far shores, is one upon which the Mexican never speculates, and which it is doubtful if he ever perceived. To him, acclimated as he has been by more than three centuries of residence in the Western world, still cling the peculiar characteristics of the Latin race. All around him has changed. The power which sent his ancestors across the sea has long since sunk under the slow disease of which old monarchies linger and die. The traditions of his country and his race are lost to him. His land has long since been invaded by Yankee dominion. He has seen the people who are here today and gone tomorrow, the weary and poverty-stricken gold hunter and the adventurer of every name and class, and they have smitten him with their vices and taught him none of their virtues. The alert and vivacious Anglo-Saxon has established himself at the principal corners in his villages; has brought him in contact with new ideas and a new language; has changed the ancient *real* and *doubloon* into paper promises, printed in green; and withal, derides his priest and laughs at his ceremonies. But through all, the Mexican clings unmoved to his religion, his language and his peculiar social life. The plough with which he tediously prepares the soil is just such a one as was used in egypt in the days of the Patriarchs. His oxen are yoked with thongs binding the straight piece of wood to the horns as was done in Virgil's time. He harvests his grain with a sickle of iron, dull and toothless as that held by Ceres herself. The wild hay upon the swale or the mountain-side he is content to cut with a hoe, and carry home upon the back of a diminutive donkey. The irregular, straggling and squalid village in which he lives is ancient beyond memory, and in its crooked streets generations of his ancestors have lived and walked, and left it unchanged. The bells which swing and jangle on an iron bar upon his church-gable, are pious gifts manufactured in Spain a hundred years ago, and presented by dead and forgotten Cardinals. The Spanish ancestor was remarkable for his highly cultivated qualities of hatred, jealousy and revenge. His descendant is remarkable only for placidity. The supreme content with which the Mexican sits upon the sheep-skin in front of his door and watches the current of surrounding life, the satisfaction he seems to take in a life which has in it only the humblest lot and the hardest fare, is nowhere else to be found in nervous, restless, wandering America.

As might be inferred, the class which comes first and oftenest under the observation of the traveller is the common one. But it must not be imagined that there are no gradations in society. Here and there through the country there are pretentious houses, whose doors are closed to the common villager, and whose Dons and Senoras hold themselves aloof from common contamination. These are the thoroughbreds, who, amid these strange surroundings, trace back a lineage which had its origin among the knights and ladies of Arragon. In this wilderness exclusiveness, what dreams of renewed Spanish power, what regrets for departed splendor, are indulged in, none know. But sometimes the necessities of life induce intercourse with the commandant of a neighboring post, or some young army officer gains admittance under cover of his uniform; and then the statements which reach a waiting world are to the effect that family greatness, as exemplified in these instances, is a myth and a dream, and exclusiveness a cloak beneath which is concealed a kind of respectable poverty.

To dance and to smoke are the two great objects of Mexican life. In the New Mexican village the sound of the guitar is always heard, and the dance is continuous. Not alone in the evening, but at midday, beneath some shade, or in an open court-yard, the passer-by stops, dances as long as he chooses, and passes on. Males and females, on whatever errand bent, join in the dance without hesitation and quite as a matter of course. It is a habit, a universal disease; the first amusement a child learns, and the last manœuvre his decrepit legs are made to perform.

Equally inveterate is the habit of smoking, and the cigarette is the universal article. Men and women alike, mingle smoke with every earthly employment. Senoras employ the intervals of the fandango in making and lighting cigarettas, and the celerity with which a Mexican manufactures the small roll of corn-husk and tobacco, never once looking at the operation, and chattering and gesticulating all the time, is astonishing.

The New Mexican village is a complete nondescript. At the distance of a mile it has the appearance of an unburned brick-kiln. The sun-dried adobe is the universal building material, and there is almost no diversity in style. No attempt is made at regularity in the streets, which are simply narrow zig-zag alleys, intended only for donkey locomotion and for the convenience of the goats. The description of a Mexican town invented by some border humorist describes them all: "Nine inches high, eighteen inches wide, and a mile and a half long." And this is really a description, so far as appearances go. The luxury of a floor, of bedsteads and chairs, is entirely unknown. Wooden doors, stoves and iron utensils are nearly so. Everything is of the earth, earthy. Beds and benches are banks of earth arranged along the walls. Fire-places are slender arches, in which the fuel is placed upright. Cooking is performed in earthenware, and the favorite and standard dish of beans is stewed two or three days in an earthen jug.

In these towns the sounds of industry heard everywhere else in Christendom are unknown. There are no shops, and every man is his own carpenter, joiner and shoemaker. Iron is the grand necessity of civilization, but here its use is scarcely known. The only wheeled vehicle the Mexican uses of his own choice is a cart which has not in it so much as a nail, and this curious triumph in the attempt to make the ugliest, heaviest and most inconvenient of earthly vehicles, goes shrieking over the mountain roads, eternally oilless.

The Mexican mode of life is agricultural, and these villages are simply gregarious collections of people pertaining to lands which are tilled in common. There is an enemy which is complacently designated as "*Los Indios*," who is constantly on the alert for spoil, and from whose incursions there is no safety save in union. Wealth here consists in a multitude of goats, together with a limited number of donkeys and oxen. In his use and treatment of these animals, the native is as peculiar as he is in other respects. Everything pays tribute to the Mexican's larder, and is included in his resources, except those things in general use among the majority of mankind. Cows are seldom milked, and goats always are; and sometimes even the small pigs go short of the mother's milk, for which, however, they cry as lustily as do infant swine the world over. Pigs, lean, noisy and miserable, are fastened to a stake by a lariat, while the donkeys are confined in pens. Dogs, innumerable and ill-favored, swarm everywhere; and domestic fowls roost among the household utensils, and lay eggs in convenient corners. Red pepper, the famous *chile colorado*, the hottest sauce ever invented, is a standard, sometimes almost an only dish, and is eaten in quantities by high and low. The manufacture of common soap is neither understood nor attempted, and its place is supplied by a plant which needs no preparation for use, and which grows wild in the country. Wood for fuel is not cut, but dug, being the huge roots of the insignificant but plentiful *mezquit*. Butter is almost unknown, but cheese made from goats' milk is a staple. There are dishes in the Mexican bill of fare of which the mere name conveys no meaning, and which are unknown to the general world of gormands and epicures. There is a drink which is the very concoction of Beelzebub, distilled from a plant which if not the same is very nearly allied to the famous centuryplant. Acrid as turpentine, fiery as proof spirits, its effect is more like insanity than drunkenness, and its use adds nothing to the agreeableness of a race who even when sober are the opposite of ingenuous.

What is a country in which the two articles leather and iron are not in general use? asks the political economist. Yet here, the use of both these articles is practically unknown. Chains, tires, straps, hinges, braces, everything which requires lightness, strength and toughness, is made of raw-hide, and the Mexican is exceedingly expert in its preparation. Applied to his uses, it is firm, strong and nearly indestructible. I have known a dozen mules to chew a long Summer night through upon a single lariat, and leave it unscathed; which to one acquainted with the perseverance of that animal in any task of the kind is sufficient testimony. The shoes of the Mexican, made of a thinner variety of the same material, always last until they share the fate of most articles of the kind in this country, and are stolen by the coyotes. Everything broken is mended with this article, and without it the common operations of life could hardly be carried on.

The primitiveness of Mexican life is more particularly displayed by the dress of the common class than by any other one sign. Stockings and gloves are an American innovation, and seldom seen. Generally neither sex is encumbered with more than two distinct articles of clothing besides the head-dress, which is with both sexes as elaborate as circumstances will admit. The females wear a short skirt and a single upper garment of a not unfamiliar pattern, in which, in maid and matron alike, at all times and places, are displayed robust arms and brown *torsos*. But no one ever caught a man without his *sombrero*, or a woman without the *rebosa*. The first named is the most elaborate article of the hat kind, profusely adorned with gold embroidery. A Mexican's hat is an article of profound importance, as indicating his respectability. It costs four times as much as his whole wardrobe besides, and more than the donkey which carries him. Shabby as he may be in other respects, his Sunday hat insures him the respect due to a well-dressed man.

The *rebosa* is a garment as old as the Spanish race, being a shawl more or less gay, and sometimes elaborate and costly, in which, in-doors and out, the Mexican woman hides her face. Shoulders, arms and feet may be bare, but all that can be seen of her countenance is one eye and her nose. Peculiarly graceful, as the females of her race are in all respects, long habit renders her especially adroit in the management of the national head-dress. Eating, smoking, talking, the *rebosa* never falls, is never blown away, and its easy folds are never disarranged. If ever in this country the traveller espies in the distance a human figure upon whose head is to be seen neither hat nor shawl, he may begin to study the means of defence, for it is no friend, but an Apache.

To the native all the beasts of the field are of small importance compared with the little donkey, called in the language of the country a "*burro.*" They are very small, many of them not so large as the smallest pony, and many a cuff and kick, bestowed in lieu of forage, from colthood up, have made them even smaller than nature intended. They are melancholy brutes, much given to forlornness of countenance and leanness of flank. Appearances indicate that with all his reverence for sacred things, the Mexican has forgotten that the *burro* carries upon his shoulders the Cross, and once played a prominent part in the most distinguished ecclesiastical procession commemorated by his own mother-church. The *burro* is tied by having a blanket thrown over his ears, and guided by vigorous thwacks of a cudgel on either side of his patient head. He is freighted with everything which can be tied upon him, and in such quantities that frequently all that is visible of him are his four little feet, and those enormous ears which in all his kind have refused to be hidden, even by a lion's skin. He is the carrier of hay, of stones, bales of goods, casks of water, and sometimes of a whole family of small children. His master has a confidence in his powers of locomotion and endurance which would honor an elephant. Burdened with humanity or merchandise, faithful of disposition, frugal of habit and tough of hide, the little slave toils through his hard life with a patience and submissiveness which make him the martyr of the brute creation.

The small commercial transactions of the Mexican remind one of the shrewd dealing of a schoolboy. Should the purchase of eggs become desirable to the traveller he must be content to buy them two, three, or half a dozen at a time. He will spend an immense amount of eloquence in attempting to convince the purchaser that they are worth fifty cents per dozen, while all the time he is anxious to take half that sum. Should milk be wanted he will swear by all the saints that the yellow and unctuous fluid is the milk of a cow, and not of the goat from whose udders it is yet warm. If it be fowls, the hoarse old master of the harem will always be pointed out as young, tender and just the bird for Senor's supper. Discovered in his small rascality, the varlet disarms resentment by a smile so bland and a shrug so expressive that you are convinced he means no harm by being an inveterate liar.

The female of every tribe and race varies from the male by a greater difference than is expressed by masculinity and femininity. But the Mexican woman is in many respects more a woman and less a heathen than could be expected from her surroundings. Always neat in attire and cleanly in person and surroundings; comely and sometimes beautiful in face and figure; always trying to look pretty, with a weak side for flattery and admiration; coquettish in her ways and suave in her manners; tender and kind to those she loves; with a laugh or a tear always at hand, as her sisters have the world over; she is in all respects a striking contrast to the surroundings of her daily life, and the habits of the country in which she lives.

And while all this is true, there comes following after it a truth which is in itself a problem for the socialist and the student of human nature. Stated as a proposition, any form of society not cemented and supported by a peculiar and almost indescribable spirit of chastity is sure to fall. Virtue must be regarded, venerated, *inherited*—taught unceasingly by the mother, the schoolmaster, and the priest. Such is not the case here. Prostitution, bigamy and adultery go licensed and shameless. Faithfulness to the marriage vow is not deemed essential to connubial peace; and the *idea* of absolute virtue is not extent. The Mexican women present the strange spectacle of almost universally modest demeanor and gentle manners, fulfilling the ordinary duties of home and life in a manner far better than could be expected from them in their ordinary course of training and education, and yet without an idea of the meaning, as it is generally understood, of the word virtue. The fact is a plain and undisputed one. Let those study it who are given to the investigation of social questions, and who believe in limited matrimonial contracts and speculate upon affinities. The train of social debauchery passes by, and the grand result comes thundering after; for a large portion of the population is more or less affected by that malady which is one of the direst strokes inflicted by the angel with the flaming sword who stands at the gate of the garden of forbidden pleasure.

No one need go to Rome to acquire a knowledge of what Catholicism is at home. The seat of the Papal Government, with the old man of infallibility throned in the midst, is not more thoroughly Catholic than is New Mexico. The passion for relics, saints, images, candles and processions is universal throughout the country. Nearly all the villages are named Saint somebody, and Jesuitism is an established rule. The worst social vices and the most degrading sins are coupled with the deepest regard for everything which smacks of saintship and sacredness. Every hamlet has its church, or a building which is erected for that purpose. Each churchyard is a Golgotha, which in some instances has been many times dug over for the purpose of burying the dead within sacred precincts. Skulls and large bones,—a cheerful sight to those whose friends have been interred there,— are piled within the railing which surrounds the grave of some occupant who has not yet been ousted from that limited freehold to which the poorest of us are supposed to be entitled at last.

Convenient appliances for the doing of penance are included in nearly every sacerdotal outfit. There are crosses large enough for practical utility, which penitents are required to carry far out among the hills and back, to atone for some unwonted sin. There are whips and ropes-ends for flagellation; and sometimes barefoot pilgrimages are required over a country where almost every step is thorny. Lighter sins are purged away by lying all night on a gravestone,—a thing at the bare idea of which the soul of the Mexican quakes within him; and sometimes by bumping the head a great number of consecutive times upon the church-steps. Whether this last-named exercise is a mere form, or whether the saving thumps are given with faithfulness and vigor, depends entirely upon the thickness of the skull and the tenderness of the Mexican conscience.

The *festas*, or sacred days, come so often and are observed so generally that the ill-natured remark has been frequently made that they were invented to avoid the necessity of work and lay the responsibility for consequent poverty upon the saints. The motley procession which parades the streets upon these occasions, firing guns, yelling and singing, behind a tawdry image of the Virgin arrayed in pink muslin, with a black silk mantilla and kid gloves, is one of the raggedest, noisiest and most ludicrous performances ever called by the name of religious.

Yet this curious form of Christianity is not wanting in its consolations. There are no free-thinkers and sceptics here. Under its influence the Mexican becomes courageous in danger and hopeful in death. In those times which frequently come in this country when his companions run in desperation from the Apache, still hoping to escape when there is no chance for life, he drops quietly upon his knees and camly dies with a prayer on his lips to that Mother of Christ whose name is dearer than all others to the Catholic heart. Nevertheless, the writer of this is reminded by the very making of the above statement to be personally thankful that the sturdy Protestant is apt on such occasions to follow an Anglo-Saxon instinct and die fighting if necessary, running if possible.

And so this curious and almost isolated people live on, content in their straggling villages and their primitive life, careless and ignorant of all things outside their limited world. They know not that the skies are changing over their heads, and that they or their children must ere long take part in the march of a great people or be left forgotten by the road-side while their places are taken by others.

Even at this distance of time and space, I recall the old familiar, lazy Summer afternoon in Mexico. I remember how the Senoritas sat with folded hands about the doors, and looked with one unveiled and furtive eye upon the passers-by. Ancient and parchment-faced crones chattered and smoked at the corners of the plaza, and impish boys played noisy games in the dusty street. The cocks and hens sauntered in and out of the owners' houses, with an air of contented ownership; and venerable and bearded goats perambulated the crumbling garden-walls. The unhappy pig whined and pulled at his tether, and kids furtively nibbled at the tail of the solemn old donkey, who stood with closed eye and hanging lip, asleep. I see the white tops of the far Sierras gleam in the slant sunshine, and gradually the long shadows creep over the scene, and there is nothing visible in the gloom but the outline of the cold peaks against the fading purple of the sky. The lights twinkle few and far between in the village street. There is no longer any sound but the tinkling of the guitar, and the laughter of the dancers —and dim and far the bleating of the flocks. All is the perfect peace of contented poverty. All is today; and there is no tomorrow.

I wonder as I recall such scenes whether I shall see the day when these dry bones shall be stirred, and these ancient fossils live again a new life. The land is already touched by the farthest ripple of the mighty wave which slowly creeps horizonward, burdened with life, energy and change. There already is the camp of the advance guard which widens the borders of the mighty civilization destined to include within its boundaries a hundred millions of freemen.

THE SCOUT'S MISTAKE.

THERE is a poor adobe house close by the brink of the *acequia*. The cottonwoods and willows which grow near the water add a little shade and comfort, but take nothing from the abiding dreariness of the spot. Behind it, up the steep hill-side, clamber the stunted cedars among the huge rocks. Over the hill, half a mile away, is the quadrangle of houses, the green parade-ground, the little hum and bustle of guard-mount and roll-call, and the great starry-and-striped banner which hangs all day in the limpid sunshine.

If the shanty and the post have any possible relation to each other, the passing stranger is unable to perceive it. There could be no more perfect seclusion in the depths of the wilderness. The straggling path among the boulders and cedars of the hill-side is seldom used. There is no sound save the echoes of the morning and evening gun to disturb the place; and the occupant, whoever he may be, wants only protection and disdains society.

You would be puzzled to know from his appearance whether the man who sits under the awning of boughs in front of the adobe be Indian or Spaniard. Whichever he may be, he is also cousin to the Anakim. Were it not for the stoop in his great shoulders, he would be several inches over the standard of ordinary men. His straight hair, slightly gray, falls upons his shoulders; his square jaws, high cheek-bones and aquiline nose are the color of mahogany; and the arms which lie listlessly

across his knees are simian in their brawny length. As
he lifts his head with a kind of growl as you approach
him, you can see that his eyes are sloe-black and small
and wicked, and the whole man bespeaks a capacity for
the doing of deeds as unscrupulous as they are daring.
If he is a Mexican he lacks the politeness of his race,
for he will not bid you the courteous " *Bueno dios,*" nor
ask you to sit down. If an Indian, he is in the wrong
place and near the wrong people. He is neither—and
both; and as a fair specimen of the admixture of Spaniard and Apache, he offers fair cause for the hope that
the two races have but seldom mingled.

There is an art which has no place among the sciences,
which the schools cannot teach, and of which the savans
know nothing, which is more wonderful in its accuracy,
more precise in its details, and more curious in its practice than much that Cuvier and Agassiz have written.
Its school is the far verge of civilization, and its disciples
ignorant sons of the wilderness. By it the dull and far-
off sounds and the intricate and unimportant signs of
nature are read as an open book, and tell strange tales.
By it the dreary and monotonous wastes of mountain
and plain are traversed with an instinct almost as unerring as that of the migratory bird. It constructs a tale
from a broken reed, and gathers a history from a dim
footstep in the sand, and its followers are the very sleuth-
hounds of humanity. It is the art of the trailer or scout,
and of these the grim inhabitant of the adobe was one of
the most famous.

Mariano owed his accurate education as much to birth
as to training, and his whole life was an evidence that
isolation and desert silence are not wanting in the incidents which sometimes make existence a curiosity. His

mother was a Mexican captive, whose name and family he only guessed, and his father an Apache dignitary, from whom this his son was captured at eight years of age. He was born in the camp of those whom he afterwards made his livelihood by hunting; and the Indian instinct, the frontier training and the quartermaster's money were the three things which made Mariano what he was. Yet not entirely, for he had certain characteristics of his own, namely: colossal strength, a wily head and strong passions.

Almost the only levity in which Mariano ever indulged was evoked by a narrative of his own capture on that early summer morning long ago, when he fell off the pony from behind a squaw and ran for cover as fast as his young legs and his Indian instinct would carry him. How a *caballero* turned aside from the pursuit and chased him, and reaching down as he rode beside him, caught him by the tuft of hair upon his head, carried him thus for some distance, and then, placing him beside an immense rock which served to mark the place, bade him wait until he returned. Mariano understood and waited. Why, none but he could explain; and certainly he never did. This was in the old days, when the Mexicans and Indians had it all to themselves; and thus began the scout's adventurous life. He dimly remembered the name and clan of his father, and the sad eyes and handsome face of his slave-mother. He had cause to remember them; but as he sits listlessly beside his lonesome cottage-door, seeming to have nothing in common with humanity, you need not ask him to tell of them. Nothing makes Mariano so furious as to question him of these things. Once he was boastful of his career. But that was years ago. He has had a revelation since then; and as all men's revelations are apt to do, it came too late.

Mariano went to live with his captors in one of the villages of the Rio Grande, and having in a short time asserted himself and repelled enslavement, was contented. But he was a different character from most of those around him, He was restless, alert, silent, and in his carelessness of society and his love of the mountains, first learned the rudiments of the strange profession in the practice of which he became noted. Among his first efforts, he followed the trail of the Apache, and hundreds of rugged miles became almost as familiar to him as the village plaza. Reckless by birth, and taught by circumstances, he learned to forget that he was allied by blood to the men he hunted. Besides, he had spent his years with the race to which his mother belonged, and their questionings recalled to him with a vividness as of yesterday the sorrowful face of the slave who bore him— beaten, spurned, driven like a beast, a stranger among fiends of her own sex, a captive and a mother. As he grew to manhood, the memory became a passion. He became remarkable for his vindictive hatred of *los Indios*, and his skill and unscrupulousness in warfare against them. Of all men, his eye was keenest, his hearing sharpest, and his head clearest; and when, at last, the great Republic sent its soldiers to occupy the land, Mariano was one of the most unscrupulous, cunning and desperate Indian fighters.

Then began in earnest the life of the scout. He was no longer required to follow the trail for love of his mother and hatred of his father alone, but at five-and-twenty was the recipient of a daily ration, and at the end of every month of twenty of the quartermaster's yellow coins.

The history of this rugged country for two centuries is the history of almost uninterrupted strife. The earliest and latest work of the military whose isolated posts stand at intervals through the land is a history of small campaigns, but seldom successful and often disastrous, against the Ishmaelite of the mountains. In one of the earliest of these expeditions by our forces, the cavalcade which filed into one of the long-since-abandoned and almost-forgotten posts, showed a grotesque addition to its numbers in a curious group of captives.

In huge baskets, slung upon either side of a donkey, were three Apache children, the larger upon one side and the two smaller upon the other. They blinked their small black eyes upon their new surroundings with an expression in which there was little change of wonder or fear, ate ravenously all that was given them, and uttered never a word. Besides these, there was a girl of fifteen, who stood apart, of whose face, as many curious eyes looked upon it that day, it seemed hard to tell whether it was beautiful or only wild and strange. The low forehead, tawny skin, and straight black hair, betrayed the Indian; but the full lips, the small nose, the oval face, and the round and graceful figure, were strange to Apache lineage. But more than all, the eyes, big and sad and bright, with the slight downward curve of the outer corners, were the historic, troubabour-sung brilliants which have been the inheritance of the gazelles and the swarthy daughters of the south, and none others, from the earliest times of poetry. Clad in rags, moccasoned and bare-headed, this child of savagery looked around her upon the first walls, the first civilization and the first white men she had ever seen with their own surroundings; showed her white teeth in a smile which betokened the realization of something she had heard or dreamed of; said slowly, "*Ah! muy grande—muy grande;*" and then covered her poor head with a corner of her scant blanket, and cried like any child.

The squaw could speak Spanish then? In that supreme moment she did. But few heard her, and they forgot the circumstance. They clothed her in decent garb and placed her among the laundresses, and these loud-voiced and kind-hearted women, whose roving fortunes had begun in the green Gem of the Sea, and whose husbands were dragoon corporals, taught her the mysteries of the rubbing-board and the smoothing-iron, and the virtues of cleanliness and calico. Truly, she learned early and well, and while they scolded and taught, they also gave her a name, a strange one for a squaw, and one to which many a blue-eyed and rosy Irish lass has answered ere now, for they called her—Kate.

But, in compliance with orders from the supreme authority at the post, they also watched. The adobe walls were high, and the guards were vigilant, but this daughter of the wilderness would be unlike her kind if she failed to use a dark night, agile limbs and Indian cunning to clamber over the barriers and return to her kindred. Therefore these Amazons were an unarmed guard, a kind of committee of safety, and were cognizant of most of the sleeping and waking moments of this lonely and bright-eyed captive, who passed her days and nights seemingly unconscious of surveillance, and who, in her daily growth in stalwart beauty and patient docility belied all the traditions of her tameless race.

But, by and by, they came to watch her less and love her more. Kate had learned to come when called and to do when bidden in the rich brogue of Cork. But she never talked and seldom laughed. In time of leisure she would sit for hours upon the ground, her back against the wall, and with her brown hands clasped upon her knees look far across the bare parade-ground and over the wall, at the blue sky and the white mountain-tops beyond and far away. And when, in the early evening, the brief signal-fire would blaze a moment and die upon the hills, Kate's eyes would glitter and her breath come quick and fast. But her dull tutors never noticed that.

Three months passed in this manner, and Mariano was taken up on the quartermaster's roll of "persons and articles" as the "hired scout," and became a resident of the post. Clad in fringed pantaloons and hundred-buttoned jacket, the frontier giant sauntered in and out among the mules, and made *cinchos* and contrived packs, and in the intervals lounged at the trader's store and gambled at monte. His situation and surroundings pleased him. He had always been more or less a hero, and now he also earned money and was in the matter of authority only less than the commandant himself. How familiar to Mariano's memory must be the blue jackets and orange trimmings and antiquated arms of the old Second Dragoons, now only known in the ancient records of the War Department, but among whose ranks once rode the Lees and Johnstons. The memories of such things are only preserved in the minds of men like him, and they are always silent. But the intricacies of the trail and the glint of arms did not dim the vision of the scout for another kind of observation, for he had a ready eye for the faces and charms of senoritas wherever he found them.

One day he invaded the by no means sacred precincts of the laundresses' quarters, and in going thither he came

upon Kate sitting upon the ground and looking away off
at the sky. He passed her and stared, and passed on,
still looking back. The first Amazon he saw he plied
with a torrent of Spanish and a whole pantomime of
gesticulations. Amazon listened and stared for a while,
and then placing the knuckles of her red hands upon her
hips, marched up to him, and obtruding her square jaws
and pug nose as nearly as she could into his very face,
bade him "Git out wid ye;" and as the scout, understanding the action if not the words, departed, she turned
again to her wash-tub, muttering "The darty Mixican,
an' won't I be tellin' the carporal av him." Mariano
passed the captive again, and stared at her in wondering
admiration, like a child at a new toy. And when he
caught her startled eye he took off his embroided *sombrero*
and bowed low, and then wondered at his own temerity
and hastened away. As for Kate, she looked after his
gigantic figure with an expression upon her face which
probably in all her life had never found place there before,
and arose and went away, more strange and silent than
ever.

Of course Mariano learned the story of the captive as
soon as he found some one who understood his questions.
But it only mystified him, being contrary to all his experience. But his keen eye watched the laundresses'
quarters as closely as ever they had watched for the trail,
and sometimes he caught a glimpse of Kate, and then he
bowed low and smiled, and she ran away. He had never
heard her speak. He concluded that she could not, and
never got near enough to her to test the matter. Somehow, had she only smiled he would have considered it the
supremest happiness. He would not have touched her
with the tip of his finger. He was a little afraid of her.

He,—afraid! Should Mariano fear a squaw? No, he did not think of it in that sense; but after all he was, because it is the same old story: Mariano was in love.

All this time there were preparations for an expedition against the common enemy. Mariano continued to go in and out among the packs, ever thinking of something else. And as he dreamed and thought, he had a lover's inspiration: he would give her something to remember him by during the long eight weeks of absence. So he lurked and watched for two tedious days, and finally managed to come upon Kate when the Amazons were absent. His big healthful heart beat very rapidly as she rose up from her seat upon the ground with a frightened look and turned to fly. But Mariano took off his hat with a deprecating gesture, and performed the pantomime which means "Now don't go—*please* don't." As she hesitated he held before her his gift, a glittering cross of barbaric, beaten gold. "Take it, Senorita," said he; "wear it for me while I am gone." There is no emblem so well understood as the symbol of the salvation of mankind; but the girl, as she looked upon it, seemed to wonder at his words. As she took it timidly in her fingers and turned it over and over, a new intelligence came into her eyes. Then she took from her bosom another cross, and held it hanging from her neck by a small string of sinew. She placed it beside the other and compared the two, still with the look of new knowledge in her face. No wonder, for these two were the only crosses Kate had ever seen.

Mariano examined the girl's one rude keepsake, and wondered within himself how she got it and why she wore it. It was a small toy carved of white bone; upon one side, not unskillfully cut, the well-known image of the Great Martyr, and upon the other, two curious letters and a date. Doubtless it was a specimen of old monastic skill carved in a cell across the sea; but why did the scout look at it so long and curiously, and still hold it and look? Because it seemed to bring back an indefinite memory of something long passed. It reminded him of a dim time when he was often hungry and often cold, and when scenes and places changed rapidly. It was associated in his mind with a leathery smell and smarting eyes, and wildness and haste. Above all it recalled a beautiful and suffering face, and kisses and caresses and tears. While he still pondered he had fastened his gift beside the other, and given them back to the girl. She turned away from him, the tears almost in her black eyes, and, seeming to forget his presence, suddenly kissed the cross she had worn, muttered the one word "Madre,"—almost as sweet in that liquid tongue as the English "mother,"—and was gone. What could she mean when she whispered "mother?" And stranger still, where could this shy Apache girl have learned the sweet significance of a kiss? The strongest associations and dearest memories of this sad life are connected with that word and that act, and poor Kate either knew them of herself or had learned them from some source not altogether consistent with her wild life and her savage ancestry.

The grotesque train of burdened asses, the gay horses prancing in utter ignorance of coming hardship, and the riders destined to return horseless, footsore, weary and in rags, filed out of the post and took its way towards the mountains. In front, beside the commandant, rode Mariano, somewhat moody, and more melancholy than he had ever been in his life before. But the probabilities and adventures of the expedition in the mountains were not uppermost in his thoughts. His memory of hidden springs, desolate passes and camping-places, was blurred and mingled with more recent mysteries. We have all seen the blustering, busy, impatient fellow, intensely occupied with the business in hand, who, when alone, and no one is looking, sits himself down in a retired corner at the depot, in the hotel, or upon the railway-car, and reads for the twentieth time the tinted sheet covered with the delicate lines of a woman's pen. How his world-worn face changes as he reads again the words already almost known literally by heart. By and by he places it again in his securest pocket, and is ready, as before, for all that comes. He seems to have forgotten it, but he has not, and to a greater or less extent it influences his life.

Mariano had no letter in his pocket, and could never have read it if he had; but he had the same feeling, the same delicious, haunting, obtrusive sensation in his heart of which the dear and foolish epistles which came to us when we were young were the fuel. And then that little worn white cross! As he watched the regular footfalls of his mule, and absently twisted the fringes upon his thigh, how often did he turn that obtrusive mystery over in his mind. He had seen it, he knew it well, and through a mist it seemed connected with rocks, and camps, and dew, and childish ideas. And the face it reminded him of—the sorrowful, patient, beautiful face! It seemed to the scout as he pondered that the only memories of his life in which tenderness had any place were somehow connected with a small white cross. And one midnight, two days afterwards, as he lay watching the filmy clouds and sailing stars, still thinking, it came to him—came with a thrill which went to his fingers' ends, and then

came surging back to his heart. It was joy at first which
made him start up from his rude bed, and then it was a
sorrow clothed in mystery which nearly drove him to
despair. Ay, that little cross, with its sad image and
date, he had last seen eighteen forgetful years ago, upon
the bosom of a woman whose homelessness and helplessness and sadness he had even then almost understood,
and whose wrongs he had during these long years avenged
with a kind of blind ferocity. *It was his mother's;* and
as he lay down again among the sleeping figures, he
wiped the clamminess from his forehead.

Even then his trained ear seemed to catch a slight
sound which was not of the camp. As he raised his
head and listened and looked, the small stone rolled down
the hill and stopped in silence at the bottom. The sentinel stood carelessly leaning upon his piece with far-away
thoughts, but a dim figure moved rapidly away in the
valley shadows. The scout was in no mood for alarms.
Starlight is deceptive, and perhaps it was only a gray
coyote. But in the early morning he stopped suddenly
in the march, and creeping upon his knees examined long
and curiously the faint footsteps in the dry sand of the
ravine. They were moccason-tracks, and they were alone.
"Indians?" said the commandant. "No," said the scout
with the pantomime which means utter perplexity. Mariano was at last puzzled in his profession, and like a
learned doctor he declined to give any opinion in a diffi-
cult case. Apaches inhabited these mountains, and they
only. But an ordinary Apache never made these footprints. See here, and here, and here—they are a woman's
steps, and *the toes are turned outward. Quein sabe?*

The night of the day upon which the scouting force
left the post, the Indian girl had been seen quietly asleep

by her mentors and guards. But when morning came, they mourned alike the absence of their husbands and their pupil. How or when no one knew; but over the wall and far away Kate was gone. There were none there who could be spared, even if they could follow so light a trail. The women could only lift their hands on high, and exclaim, "Did ye's iver?" and return to their washing; and by none of them was she ever seen again.

It were useless to recount the incidents of the weary, thirsty days of an unsuccessful scout. Everywhere the phantom Indian vanished from the freshest trail. They seemed near, but never to be overtaken. The troopers' horses flagged and died, and even the donkeys grew sore, weary and stubborn. After four weeks the ragged and disheartened command turned backward over the bald hills and arid plains, through canons that had lain voiceless as their stones for centuries, and by valleys so green and smiling that they seemed the Edens of an uninhabited world. Since then the experience has been a thousand times repeated, and is as old to the American regular as the manual of arms.

One night the camp lay in tired sleep in the mountain starlight, brilliant almost as the moonlight of thicker atmospheres. The post was less than fifty miles away. Discipline relaxed, the sentinel, ragged and tired, sat nodding upon a rock. Now and then a coyote, anticipating the feast of the morning, looked treacherously over the rocky ledge, and retired and chattered to his companions. The rabbit looked curiously at this new invasion of his wilderness, and laying his long ears down, bounded noiselessly away. Of all the seventy tired men, there was but one who took note of these things. Mariano lay tired and restless looking at the stars. How many strange things had lately occurred to disturb the scout's healthful life, he alone knew, and he was even now thinking of the morning when near the same spot he had found the footsteps in the sand. A new and disturbing influence had come upon him. But this meditating frontiersman little knew how much his heart had to do with it.

Suddenly his alert senses caught a sound. Not the barking of the coyote, or the timid gallop of the rabbit. Thump, thump, thump,—faint and dull, but still a definite and intermittent sound. They who have lain in frontier camps could hardly fail to recognize it from its very suggestion. It was the driving of a picket-pin. So dim and muffled it was that none but the scout would have heeded it. And it was not the sound that was strange, but the circumstance; and Mariano knew as he listened that it was the Apache's wooden pin driven with a stone. Then he rose up stealthily, and so noiselessly that none heard him, and took his gun and crept away. Every sense was alert and keen as the tiger's when he watches for his prey. What, he thought, if after all the expedition should not be unsuccessful. The sound ceased, and he crouched upon his knees and slowly crept on. Then he waited and listened, and now the sound that came to his ears was one which only he would have heard or recognized—the faint tearing, crackling whisper, with, at long intervals, a slow, dull footstep. It was that sign which not even an Indian can prevent—a pony, grazing. He must be near now; the gray dawn is breaking in the east, and moments are hours. As the scout crept nearer and peered over the low rocks he saw the pony grazing at the end of his tether, and a figure,—were there two? —seated upon the ground. As he watched them he saw that they were few, and wondered as much as he had at the footprints. Had Indians lost all cunning, or had he? He grew tired of waiting and rose up and walked rapidly down the slope towards them. Then two figures, indistinct in the morning gray, darted away up the opposite slope, one of them leading the other by the hand, The instinct of the Indian-hunter was strong in him, and the thirst for the blood of his game came upon him. Without a thought of the fateful consequences of the swift messenger to him, he raised his gun, and with one hasty glance along the barrel, fired upon the retreating figures. The hindermost fell, and as the echoes of the shot died away on the desert stillness the scout drew near the victim of his skill.

There in the gray light lay a woman whose long gray hair was tangled in the coarse grass. Her face was worn and wrinkled with the suffering of years, but in the pallid features and the dying eyes was something far from Indian origin. It was a poem,—a story of faded beauty and long waiting, melting at last into the shadows of death. And beside her knelt the other, a shapely creature whose eyes were full of tears, and whose hand trembled as she held before the filmy eyes a small white cross, beside which glittered one of yellow gold.

When at last, awakened by the shot, the soldiers came, the dare-devil scout lay prone upon the earth beside a corpse. His face was hidden upon the dead breast, and while his strong frame was convulsed in agony, his big brown hand caressed his mother's pallid face. And Kate,—poor, innocent, ignorant Kate,—born in the wilderness, but gathering nevertheless something of that knowledge which only mothers teach, who had used her captivity to learn where and how to bring her mother back and herself to return to her lover, and with the cunning learned of her wild life had followed close upon the trail of the white men for security from pursuit by her own kindred, sat and looked upon the scene, the cross in her hand, and her big eyes full of wonder and horror and grief.

The very plainest life has in it may strange events, but it would be sad indeed if the loves and sorrows which come to us all, ever resulted as the story-makers would fain have them. The clouds pass, the sunshine comes at last, and we find that of life's cup the very lees are sweet. The half-breed girl learned afterwards to understand more fully the meaning of the symbol which had been her mother's one poor keep-sake of home, happiness and religion, and how she was the second child of captivity. She had many a lover afterwards, but never a brother. Long ago the mother of swarthy sons, she tells to the youngest on her knee the curious story of the camp and the captivity, and shows him a small white cross. But she leaves out of the story the sad death upon the hillside, and says nothing of the remorseful and gloomy hermit, who, far in the hill-country sits beside his door, bankrupt in all the ties of kindred and love, and striving still in the very luxury of vindictiveness, to quench the remorse in his heart, and wash out in many an Indian's life-blood, the stain upon his own red hands.

COPPER-DISTILLED.

THOSE have been masterly efforts of romance which, without any foundation in truth, have created the widely accepted picture of the ideal American Indian. When confronted with the actual hero, the creations of Cooper cease to attract, and, indeed, become in that sense ridiculous. Lordly, eloquent, brave, faithful and truthful, he made those sons of the forest whose scattered children now linger upon coveted reservations, and in worthlessness and squalor await final extermination. Filthy, cunning, cowardly, treacherous and thievish, are their near relations who still wander in independence west of us. Every tradition repeating the story of Indian bravery, generosity and hospitality fades like mist before the actual man. The instinct of baseness runs through the whole family, from King Philip and Red Jacket down to Sa-tan-te and he of the variegated continuation. The common incidents of savagery are intensified in the race. Brave only in superior numbers or under cover; honest only in hypocrisy; merry only at the sight of suffering inflicted by his own hand; friendly and hospitable only through cunning; and sublimely mendacious always, the Indian as he is actually known seems poor material out of which to manufacture a hero, or frame a romance. All the efforts made in his behalf have failed generally to change his status or alter his life. Prominent as he has always been in American history; always the impediment to be removed, and afterwards the dependant to be supported; mollified by semi-annual gifts, oiled and pacified by periodical talks about the Great Father and blarney about "brothers;" through campaigns, councils, treaties and tribal reservations, he has come at last to within a few years of the end of his race, with only the one redeeming fact upon his record, that he has never been thoroughly tamed, and has never been a servant. Neither has the hyena.

The reservation Indian is no curiosity. The red blanket, the variegated shirt, the shanky legs and the barbaric jewelry are recognized daily on the street. But the details of an unsought and early relinquished acquaintance with the wilder tribes of the Plains and mountains may more probably contain here and there an item of interest.

If you know the Indian of Eastern Kansas, you need have no difficulty in recognizing his brother of the Plains. The family resemblance is complete. Stolidity, silence, and an indifference which passes for dignity, are the noticeable features. The camp is the epitome of Indian domestic life. There is the "tepe," or lodge, from which was taken the idea of that famous and cumbersome tent which is connected with every one's recollections of the first year of the war. Of the two, the Indian's is the better tent. Those white, neatly-sewed skins which form the cover represent many weeks of hard squaw labor, and the many poles, worn and smooth by constant dragging, came from the mountains hundreds of miles away. Within this is gathered all there is of Indian wealth and comfort. Around the walls are arranged the piles of furs which are the beds of a numerous family, and which, in the intervals of occupation, are usurped by a horde of dogs. The fire of "chips" is kindled in the centre, and the smoke is left to find its way out because of the interior being too full to hold any more. Between the irregular rows of tents straggle the unoccupied population,—children, young men and warriors. Dangling from saddles, tied to saplings, hung upon every available projection, are pieces of buffalo-meat, the whole sum of the ordinary commissariat, in all stages of odorous decay.

Everywhere and always, the men are idle and the squaws at work. The ancient crone,—gaunt, haggard and toothless,—is never old enough to be idle. To her lot falls all the endless labor of a nomadic life. Her position for all time is that of a slave. She is whipped, abused, driven like a beast of burden. She is bought and sold as a chattel; and even her Indian education is limited to one lesson,—to toil and be silent. Nevertheless, in all that is peculiarly Indianesque, she excels her teachers. In cunning, hatred and revenge, in the specialties of cruelty and the refinements of torture, she has no equal on earth. The saddest fate which awaits the captive is to be given over to the squaws.

There is no more beauty extant among Indian "maidens," than there is among the gorillas. Never were the ugly features which pertain to the unmixed race modified for beauty's sake. More wonderfully false than even Cooper's tales, are the poems which descant upon the charms of dusky love. Poetic license is a wanton and wayward thing, and has been made to caper nimbly to strange tunes ere now. But the man who invented Indian idealism, and clothed the ragged, wretched, brutal, insect-haunted squaw with love, and did it awake and knowingly, ought to have been born early enough to have followed Dante on his sulphurous pilgrimage, and not have returned.

It is an experience probably not to be objected to for once, but a repetition of which is not desirable, to watch for an hour the operations going on in this aggregation of unwashed humanity. There is the young squaw, who has become the possessor of some flour, and who is engaged in transforming the same into bread. She has a small fire, a battered iron pan, and near by is a pool of muddy water. She pours in a quantum of water, and stirs the mass into proper congruity. Presently she wipes her fingers upon her encrusted blanket, and places the cakes in the ashes. Near by sits an old woman, preparing a freshly-killed carcass for that process after which it is "jerked" beef. She sits upon the ground, surrounded by every variety of animal remains. Her task is to cut the whole carcass into long thin strips for drying. But the operator is the principal curiosity. Gray-haired, wrinkled and haggard, her dried limbs scarce concealed by rags, she is the very picture of toiling wretchedness. You may stand for an hour regarding these two persons, you may laugh, question and gesticulate, and they will not betray by sign or look the knowledge of your presence.

If you would see the very pink of *hauteur* and personal pride, do but regard yon gaunt and greasy son of the wilderness, who is as much an adept in style as any of the mistaken scions of civilization. He is as unconscious of his odors as though redolent of *patchouli*. He is unwashed, and nearly naked save in the respect of paint, and if the impolite truth must be told, swarming with that industrious insect to which the Scottish poet wrote an apostrophe. He regards you with folded arms, and defiant face, and would fain impress you with the opinion that he is indeed "heap."

In Indian society, every family is the producer of all articles required in daily life. Clothing, food and weapons are all manufactured from the original material.

Barter and exchange were introduced by white men, except so far as so many ponies and robes purchased a wife; and left to themselves, each family is self-supporting, and comprises in itself the whole plan of patriarchal government. Resources are few, and in this or any camp, may be seen in an hour the whole system of Indian economy. There are the squaws who bring fuel and water, and others engaged in the long and tedious process of stretching and scraping that finally produces the white, pliable and elaborately ornamented robe, which is the representative of Indian comfort and wealth. In these processes there is nothing wasted. Every sinew is saved. Indian hunting is not pleasure-seeking slaughter, but necessity. He is as cautious of the waste of life among the herds of the Plains, as the white man is of the thrift and well-being of his tame herds, and for the same reason; from the buffalo, aided with a little wood, all his life's necessities are capable of being manufactured.

Indian life is full of pomp and ceremony, and in every camp, while the women toil stolidly, the men are engaged in some ceremony which is necessary for the proper celebration of their feats in arms or their success in future enterprises. The indian is a great braggart, and he who can boast loudest and longest is the greatest man. It is to obtain an opportunity for this that a "dance" of some kind is always in progress. Their names and purposes are nearly innumerable, and the candid uninitiated is not able to perceive any great difference in the screams, leaps and horrible hootings which characterize them all. Some of these dances are said to be religious; but all there is of religious sentiment is condensed in the word "medicine." Everything in Indian life belongs to one of two classes; it is either good or bad medicine. Camping-places where some calamity has befallen them are ever afterwards avoided as "bad medicine." The days and places which witnessed some defeat in arms are classed in the same category; and all things which are fortunate are classed upon the opposite side. The high-priest of this religion is the celebrated "medicine-man." I do not know what are the necessary qualifications for this high calling, but am forced to confess that the only perceivable difference between him and his fellows is that he is, if possible, raggeder, lazier and dirtier than they.

You would naturally infer that begging would be incompatible with the Indian character. By no means; he is the most persistent and importunate beggar on this continent. Governmental discipline has taught him that every white man owes him something, and that he ought to have it. Failing in this, he immediately wants to "swap." Among the chattels offered in exchange is frequently his squaw. The white man's inability to see the advantages accruing from this business operation seems to the Indian a peculiar trait. One of the strongest evidences of idiocy, to him, is the well-known fact that he can get more for a robe, a pony, or even a paltry bow-and-arrow, than he could for a whole family of squaws.

The language of the Indian is peculiar. Any man can "talk Indian"—not *speak* it,—who has any skill in pantomime. The comparatively few words they use are coarse and guttural. The mellifluous Indian names of mountains, streams and towns must not be taken as specimens of the dialect. In lieu of words they use signs, and mainly depend upon them for communication, even among themselves. A class of deaf mutes are hardly more expert than they in communicating ideas without sounds. I have *seen* long conversations carried on between some very communicative specimens of copper color, and army officers, only prefaced by the word "how,"—which the Indian takes as a compendium of all it is necessary to know of English. A circular motion of the hand over the head indicates a day; a jog-trot movement indicates a horse; and the two together indicate a day's journey. A still different movement of the hand denotes a buffalo,—indicating in a way not to be misunderstood the peculiar gait of that animal. Numbers are indicated by rapidly throwing up the fingers, displaying as many as answers to the number to be expressed. Of course there are words enough in the various dialects to express all those things common to Indian life, but the pantomime is always used as an indispensable adjunct.

There are many ideas extant concerning Indian skill and cunning which are incorrect and extravagant. The trapper and hunter of the Far West, the *Voyageur*, and, indeed, most of those men whose tastes lead them to follow a frontier life, are capable of outwitting the Indian in almost every instance. The trade they learn from him, they excel him in. Of course the Indian is possessed largely of the talent of stealth, being by nature and necessity a hunter. He has an instinct of cunning, which has sometimes been dignified by the name of strategy; but in his operations against his white competitors he knows nothing of that kind of strategy which is a degree nobler than lying. He can cover his head with earth and lie among the rocks at the roadside, and concealing his sinister visage by his strategy, speed an arrow after the unwary traveller. He can occupy thirty-six hours, as I have known him to do, in crawling a few rods distance to steal a mule, and finally succeed in his purpose. He will smoke the pipe, which is the universally recognized emblem of peace, with many signs of amity and many pacific grunts, and the same day lance you in the back. He will be at great pains to make a false trail. He will imitate the sounds of nature, and by a thousand devices attempt to mislead. But he has not a fraud in his whole repertory in which the white man has not long since learned to outwit him.

The few white men who have abandoned civilization and race for Indian society, aiding him by a white man's knowledge of his race in their expeditions, are leaders, not followers. It is superfluous to add that they are the more dangerous of the two, and have just sufficient humanity left to cause them to choose rather to reign in hell than serve in heaven.

The faculty of reading the face of nature, so common on the frontier, is one which we are apt to consider an instinct. To the Indian, the light step of the antelope is as plain as the track of a tornado. He tells the number and kind of his enemies, and the hours since they passed. He invented a system of telegraphy before the days of Morse, and the smoke upon the distant hill, or the brief fire upon the mountain-side, conveys to him information which he never misunderstands. He traverses the monotonous surface of a vast wilderness, and with an instinct as unerring as that of the bison reaches his destination. He hovers for days upon the path of his enemy, always near and always watching, but never seen or heard save by those who have learned his art. All these things the white man has stolen from him, and, as is usual in evil teachings, even excels his tutor. There are a large number of men on the frontier who gain a livelihood by outwitting the Indian at his own game.

It is a mistake to regard the weapons of the Indian as rude and inefficient, and to wonder how he managed before the introduction of fire-arms. The ancient bow-and-arrow, probably the first study in the science of projectiles, used in all climes and races, is now, in the hands of an Indian, one of the most effective of weapons. The wiseacres of civilization ridicule Benjamin Franklin's mistake in recommending that the Colonial troops should be supplied with this weapon. As usual, the genius of common sense was right, for it is infinitely more convenient and effective than a Queen Anne musket. By the Indian it is used in its common form, and is simply a piece of elastic wood, supplied with a string made from sinews. The arrow is sometimes an elaborate specimen of handicraft. It is about twenty-eight inches in length, elaborately feathered and ornamented. The ornamentation is peculiar to the tribe, and the head is of iron, sometimes of flint, and is fastened to the wood by a very neat and ingenious wrapping of fine sinew. This slight and fragile shaft will transfix the huge body of the buffalo, coming out upon the other side. It penetrates where the huge modern bullet is flattened or turned aside. It is noiseless, and at twenty yards seldom misses its mark. Once wounded, there is small chance of recovery, for the dried sinew relaxes in moisture, and the wood comes away and leaves an inextricable triangle of iron behind.

Indian fighting is not the placid and trifling thing it is sometimes imagined to be. The Plains Indian is a master of horsemanship. He rides upon a stuffed pad or blanket, and the surcingle or girth is furnished with a loop on each side, in which upon occasion he inserts his foot and thus hangs upon that side of his horse which is opposite his enemy, almost entirely concealed. Rapidly riding in a circle, he discharges his arrows under his pony's neck, or over his back. The Indian idea of strategy is to harass, to exhaust resources and draw premature fire. To this end he is constantly in motion, here and there like a flash. But of late years his tactics need a revision. As usual, his white adversaries have learned more of him than he knows himself. The modern soldier, trained in the mysteries of the skirmish-drill, quietly drops down in his place at the bugle-call, and from those weapons which are a triumph of celerity, accuracy and force, speeds after his foe the messenger which weighs an ounce and a half, and which, singing as it goes, tumbles many a savage rider nine hundred yards away.

This is Plains fighting. There is another system in vogue among the mountains in New Mexico. There all is concealment. There is no sound, and from behind the rocks in the canon, or concealed among the sage-brush and cactus, the arrow is sped which cuts short many an unconscious life. The Indian dead and wounded are never left on the field. A pride which is natural enough, makes it desirable that his losses should not be counted, and his scalps should not be taken, to be danced and exulted over.

The name of Great Spirit figures largely in all reports of Indian oratory, just as the name of Deity is freely used in the stirring appeals of second-class politicians. The Great Idea is as much a myth to the one as to the other. The system of theology which prevails among the Indians is merely a superstitious fear of something they cannot understand. In common with every race, the Indian believes in the immortality of the soul, and in a hereafter. What kind of heaven or hell he has imagined for himself, no man can tell. There are no strictly religious forms extant among them, and nothing that is regarded as especially sacred. The religious idea is far from prominent, and seems almost entirely included in the "medicine" business, heretofore referred to. Superstition is a different thing, and of that there is plenty. As instances, when a horse is stolen, each man must strike him at least one blow; when a traveller is murdered, each gallant participant in the honor must leave at least one arrow in the body of the victim.

Of course, in speaking of the Indian, the common class is the criterion; but, as is well-known, the red race is not without its prominent examples of force, dignity and comparative greatness. King Philip, Tecumseh and Billy Bowlegs are already historic characters. Sa-tan-te and some of the other Chiefs who met Hancock in council in 1866 were in their way remarkable men. In them, at least, the common farce of Indian dignity was condensed into something like the genuine article. The Indian stands in no awe of dignitaries, for his firm conviction is that the meanest of his race stands at the head and front of all created intelligence. It is a national egotism, like that of the Chinese. When he goes to Washington, and attracts attention, and is interviewed and stared at, he thinks it is because he is great and envied. In his mental constitution he entirely lacks the faculty of appreciation. He knows that the telegraph wires "whisper" strange stories in the ears of the white man, and that insensate paper "talks," but the knowledge of these things induces no respect for the people who make use of them. He accepts them as facts, and wonders at them as much as dignity permits; but the idea that they are any evidence of knowledge superior to his, never enters his mind.

With the old story of barbarity, cruelty and rapine, the world has long been familiar. Let no man imagine in the simplicity of his heart, and in his charity for "the poor Indian," that the story has been exaggerated. Indian atrocities which have come directly to the knowledge of the writer, truthfully delineated, are unfit for the ears of civilized mankind. It would be nearly impossible for any man acquainted personally with the history of the last six years upon the Plains to look his neighbor in the face and calmly tell what he has seen. Upon the Indian question, the Government, at its very heart and centre, is divided against itself. The costly and intricate machines of two great internal departments are running in opposition to each other. The greater portion of the army is sent to the frontier for the sole purpose of fighting Indians. Every incentive to vigilance and unceasing effort is used. Naturally there can be no playfulness or indirection in military affairs. The training of every soldier is to the effect that war is *war*, conducted with unremitting energy. In fighting Indians, as in every other case, if this be not the understanding, inculcated and enforced by every order, then the frontier is better without protection. But the Indian Bureau has a different understanding. In one district or department, an Indian campaign is being carried on with vigor; and in the adjoining district or department, they are being fed and furnished with arms, and frequently the same tribe is the recipient of both systems of treatment. So long as there remains in the system the element of miltary force, there should be no attempt to introduce also the incompatible element of persuasion. I believe there was never before an instance of a government at the same time feeding, coaxing and fighting its enemies. Something of the kind was tried during the first eighteen months of the last war, and, it is now generally thought, failed to be the proper medicine for the complaint. The peace upon the Plains is the result, solely, of a vigorous winter's military campaign.

This is an ultra-Missouri view of the case, but, as in the South-west at least, peace and safety are still in the distance, and theory and necessity still at war with each other, the banks of the Rio Grande seem as fair a standpoint from which to judge the case as the banks of the Hudson or Potomac.

In any event, the Indian is doomed. The inscrutable purpose for which he was created is almost accomplished. On general grounds, it is much better that he should go. A slight personal acquaintance is sufficient to convince any one that he lacks the instinct of self-preservation. He would rather be aggressive and die, than be peaceful and live.

It matters not that in the midst of ease and safety good men have leisure to write humanitarian letters, thousands of miles from where scalps are lifted without regard to the peaceful wisdom and high purposes they cover. The land trespassed upon belongs to the Indian, and he is justified in resistance. Granted. For so did once New England belong to him. And once all belonged to Adam. But there is no freehold save under the laws of civilization. In the time to come, the territory of the world will be lawfully claimed only by those who use it for God's first purpose, the tilling of the soil. Theorize as we may, the westward march of civilization, with all its attendant evils and final results, is the foreordination of the Almighty, and in this piece of bad theology but stubborn fact, lies the final solution of the Indian question.

JACK'S DIVORCE.

HOW Black Jack came to be sent out upon his adventures bestridden by so ill-sounding a name, never transpired, and if he ever possessed a civilized, Christian name, no one in those parts had ever heard it. He was a man thoroughly educated by the frontier; and simplicity of character, personal courage, and dog-like faithfulness were to him natural gifts.

He was not black, and except that he had upon him the ineffaceable marks of sun and wind, would have been more than ordinarily fair. His hair was a reddish brown, and his keen blue eyes had that steady and unflinching gaze which bespeaks in its owner honesty without blemish, and vision without flaw.

It is not enough to say merely that Jack was a frontiersman, because in some instances that only expresses an accident, and not a character. He had that something about him which, while it can only exist on the border, is yet a part of the man. Though not a negative man, he was one of those of whom a clearer idea can be obtained by saying what he was not, than what he was. There is a whole world in which all the famous and remarkable, and nearly all the disgraceful and mean, transactions of mankind are performed, of which Jack knew nothing.

Women, in all the splendor of pearls of the ocean and gems of the mine, endowed with all the refinements of civilization, and the tact and delicacy born of cultivated life,—bland, bewitching and fearfully and wonderfully made up,—he had never even seen. Femininity conveyed no such idea to him. The women he knew were only women in the broad sense in which female is not male. The wharfs and depots of crowded cities, the throng of the pavement and the exchange, the crowd and jam and bustle of trade, broad fields and paved roads, were all crowded out of his conceptions of life and men, and he had no speculations and opinions to digest concerning them. He had never heard the sound of church bells, and luckily for him, was entirely ignorant of the fateful differences in creeds which exist among those who diligently seek after the truth.

In his ignorance of all that is fashionable, and most that is bad among civilized mankind, he was even ignorant of the praises and luxuries men sometimes earn by dying; and the velvet turf and shaded aisles, the fair monuments and flattering epitaphs, of Greenwood or Olivet would have filled him with astonishment. His was the rock-piled and lonely grave of the wilderness, and he never dreamed that a palace was necessary to the welfare of mouldering clay.

If the schoolmaster was ever abroad in Western Arkansas, where Jack first saw the light, the benign influence never reached his mind. He could not read, and was innocent of the primary rules of arithmetic, and everything else in the way of books. The immense literature of fiction and newspaperdom was something he had hardly heard of—and yet, (the fact is stated as a redeeming one,) he knew, traditionally as it were, some of Watts's hymns, and could repeat them with the same unction and pathos with which the childish and immortal lines are repeated by nearly all who speak the English tongue.

But Jack was not a grown-up child. He lacked none of the grand essentials which go to make up the curious biped whose ancestor was an ape and whose future is— doubtful. He spoke the mother tongue with a fluency equal to the requirements of his life, and he spiced and strengthened it with that piquant slang which expresses so much in a few words that it is a pity it is considered vulgar to use it. His most peculiar characteristic, however, was not an educational one. It consisted in the almost total absence of personal fear. Whole armies of men, surging masses which number many thousands, may, and often do, go through a long day of carnage without any instance of cowardice. But this is not the kind of courage he possessed. He limped, had lost a finger, and carried an ugly scar on his cheek. But all these had been obtained at different times, and all in Indian fights. But not for glory. With no particular interest at stake, pecuniary or otherwise, he still wandered through the canons and over the hills, alone, and solely bent on killing the game he loved to hunt; apparently unmoved by repeated encounters and former escapes. Unless questioned, he said nothing of his adventures. He seemed to be ignorant of any manner of life in the conditions of which was included the common essential of personal safety.

Nor was Jack an unsocial or solitary man. While he possessed the knowledge to go anywhere through a vast wilderness, he still availed himself, when he could, of the society of his fellow men. He was employed as a laborer in and around the ranch of one Newman, near a military post. He was faithful and hard-working, and in the course of his duty undertook alone to plough and sow in wheat a piece of land, twenty miles from any house, and

in a country much prized and persistently defended by
the Apaches. He worked with his revolvers upon his
belt and his rifle in his hand. He fought the prairie fire,
always a fearful enemy in the wilderness, which his enemies had lighted to consume his cabin. He watched his
mules night after night, sleepless and undismayed, to save
them from capture, when he knew that his inveterate
enemies were near. And when the final and decided attack came, he drove his team before him, and defended
them from behind; finally got them into the cabin where
he slept, barred the door and drove off a score of Indians
by firing through the chinks of the house, and finally
came off victor, though wounded.

There is a certain fire-arm, which all have seen, and
with which many are familiar. The name of the inventor
has gone down to posterity with something very like
renown. Skilfully handled, this weapon is one which
few like to face. It is a small arsenal of rapid and sudden death, and a single man, skilled in the use of Colt's
revolver, is almost equal to six men, each armed with a
weapon which fires but a single shot. In the use of this
pretty toy, Black Jack was a miracle, even among his
skilful companions. Without any deliberation, he would
discharge a dozen shots, with a rapidity and certainty
fearful to contemplate in connection with the soft and
penetrable quality of human tissue. He was a walking
mitrailleur. Those two play-things of his, worn smooth
by constant use, never left his person, and in his pouch
he carried two extra cylinders ready for insertion.

This was one reason why Jack was not afraid of Indians.
There was no moment when eye and ear were not alert,
and the hand was always ready. He frequently remarked:
"They aint got me yit; a man can't die nohow till his

time comes." And in that last piece of philosophy he lived and believed with so profound and simple a faith that it seemed a pity it had no more sense in it.

But simple and honest as was the life of this gentle savage, he had one trouble, and that, of course, had a woman and love in it. It was the one incident which made him seem like the men around him, and showed how nearly of the same stuff we are all made.

Dolores was the handsomest woman Jack had ever known in his wild life. She was Spanish, had been as fair as a brown-colored nymph, and was still as coquettish as it runs in her race to be, and as false as the profane word Shakspeare uses as a comparative. She was only a laundress at the post, but her eyes were black and her teeth were white, and she caught Jack on the tender side which all such men present to a woman's blandishments.

Bold as he had been in his latest Indian fight, he must needs surrender to this fragile Senorita while recovering from his wounds. Dolores had had many lovers. She could hardly count them on her fingers. Some she had discarded, to-wit: all she had ever had, at odd times, of her own race; and some had discarded her, namely: certain American Lotharios who could be faithful long to none. But she was not broken-hearted, nor indeed inconsolable, and had steadily replaced vacancies by new recruits. And last came honest Jack, whose heart she accepted without hesitation, and whose money she spent without remorse. Doubtless for her sake Jack would have left off risking his life among the Apaches. There is no telling but that he might in time have been induced to live in a town, and to sleep upon a bed.

Now it must be understood in this case, as in all others of the kind, that a man's liking for a woman is not controlled by any trait in her character. Dolores was handsome, she knew men very well, and she practised the art of coquetry with all the skill of her race and her sex. It may be that there had descended to her through a long and forgotten line some of the cunning graces and charms which long ago distinguished the dames of old Castile. She had at least the softness, the subtle, smooth suavity, which gives to the women of the Latin race a peculiar attractiveness to the bluff Anglo Saxon.

So she married the hunter, after the manner of the country; and well it was, to one whose vows sat with such habitual lightness, that the ceremony was of no more binding a character. In was *bona fide* to Jack, however, and they two lived together in a small adobe, within sight of the flag-staff. Likely Dolores never intended to cling with any great tenacity to him alone. She probably argued that it was convenient, and judging him by her standard, she calculated upon his roving life, and the faithlessness of men in general, for final freedom when some new inducement offered. But as stated, it was a part of Jack's personality to be faithful. He had no idea but that he was tied hand and foot, and, as was natural, he expected a reciprocity of feeling.

In a few weeks Dolores began to use her fine eyes upon the uncouth masculines she met, after the old fashion, and Jack began to grow moody, and to look hard and determined out of his blue eyes; and by and by there was a look about him that the veriest death-seeker in all that abandoned country would hardly have cared to face, and when at home, he certainly kept his house and his family to himself.

But now there came and stayed at the trader's store, a man who wore barbaric gold and a linen shirt; one whose fingers were long, and exceeding nimble in dealing cards, and whose eye had in it a look of mingled bravado and cunning. He came as a traveller, but stayed for weeks; and ere long he and Jack's wife were exchanging glances of recognition. Fraud and cunning were so plainly written on this man's face that it was easy to believe that to defraud Jack was what he stayed and waited for.

But meantime the hunter had ideas and purposes of his own, and with a silence that was at least ominous kept his own counsel. He seemed always waiting and watching for something; and the man who has many a time waited and watched among the rocks, and many a time come off victor through vigilance, does not wait and watch for nothing. What he waited for finally came, and with it, his idea of reparation and justice.

As was not uncommon, he took his gun and canteen, and went away to the mountains. But he went regularly, and generally returned on the third day. Strangely enough, he brought back no game, but he looked clay-begrimed and tired. He told his wife when he would return on all these occasions, and so far as could be known found everything, to use his own expression, "reg'lar." Nevertheless it was a well-known fact among the knowing ones, that the dull hours were beguiled by the gambler at Jack's cabin, in these frequent absences of the owner. More than a month passed in this way, and Jack's eye grew harder and colder every day. No common man could have passed unquestioned. But there was that purpose in his face, and that determined method in his going and coming, that those who knew him well silently awaited results. Meantime, possessing all the qualities which are valued and admired in the country in which he lived, and having been faithful to all, and wronged none, he had many friends, and his enemy, if as yet he might be called such, had none.

Several times was the gambler warned that there might come a day of reckoning, but he considered himself "in luck," in that he had so simple an enemy, and he stayed on. He did not know his man. He might have known him, had he reflected that men that are cool and steady and silent are always to be feared when the time of reckoning comes with an enemy. More than once, when Jack was absent on his fruitless expeditions to the mountains, a tall figure which looked like his had been seen near his cabin in the starlight, only to glide away and disappear in the gloom.

One starry October night, when Jack had been gone only since the morning, he suddenly walked in among the story-tellers and poker-players at the store. All turned toward him with inquiry and surprise in their faces. He looked fairly grim, and there was a distinct and palpable determination on his face. He closed the door carefully behind him. "Boys," said he, "come along with me now, and I'll answer once for all the questions you've been *lookin'* at me for more'n a month; and providin' I don't do nothin' desperit, will you promise not to interfere?"

A half-looked and half-spoken answer was given, and four men started out with Jack. At the door he untied a donkey, such as are of common use in the country, and drove him before him toward the cabin. The hunter walked resolutely on, and without ceremony pushed open the door and entered. At the same moment, with the dexterity of long practice, he whipped out of its scabbard the inevitable revolver; with three strides he was across the room, and in a moment the monte-dealer was looking straight down the bore, with an expression of face which indicated that he regarded it as being several inches in diameter.

"Now," said Jack, in the peculiar tone which admitted no doubt as to its earnestness, "*my* time has come. You or I die here to-night, or you and this woman git up and go with me. Mister, you ought to know me. If you want to shoot, you kin hev a chance, but I'm apt to hit, and I'll *try*, so help me Christ!"

This fearful adjuration was uttered, not as the common profanity of an angry man, but in a tone and manner that gave it a fearful meaning. "Git up!" said he, as the gambler, with paling face, seemed about to say something conciliatory. He arose instantly. "Now"—for the first time addressing the woman—"git yer traps together. Quick!" he thundered, as she hesitated; "you shall hev your lover's company from this night to all eternity!" Though a scene in which the comic was not altogether wanting, there was still something terrible in it. The woman, her olive roses blanched with vague terror, moved nervously about, gathering her apparel into a bundle. The gambler glanced furtively at his own revolver lying on the table, and toward the door. But Jack's eye was upon him, and the implacable weapon was in his hand. Finally he placed his hand in his bosom, and drew forth a plethoric belt, opened it, and poured some of the shining pieces in his hand. Frightend as she was, the old glitter came into the woman's eyes as she saw it. There was no situation in life in which the clink of the doubloons would not be music to her. But Jack's face only changed to a look of intense contempt, as his enemy pitifully offered him first the handful, and then the belt. He was again mistaken in his man.

When the woman stood with her bundle in her hand, Jack pointed to the open door, and bade her and the gambler move out together. He caused the woman to mount the diminutive donkey, and the gambler walked behind.

Straight up toward the mountain they started, the implacable husband taking the gambler's weapon from the table as he left the room. Away in the gloom the strange procession passed, and as the donkey picked his careful way among the stones, plodding safely and patiently after the manner of his kind, the last sounds the bystanders heard were the wailing and sobbing of the woman, the stumbling footsteps of the gambler, and behind all, Jack's long and steady stride. And these died away in the distance; and in the silent gloom of the night the witnesses to the strange scene stood at the door of the deserted cabin, and looked in each other's faces, silent, and wondering.

After four days Jack returned empty-handed. He was questioned now, for human curiosity cannot be restrained forever. A grim humor was in his face, as he said, "I've purvided fur 'em. They've meat enough fur three weeks." Adding, "Any uv you as was fond of Nimble-fingers, air informed that he was well when I kim away, on'y *ruther* lonesome. But you won't see him ag'in *soon*. He aint mountain man enough to find his way back here, and I reckon he'll *hev* to fight now."

Jack thereupon cleaned his pistols, got together such things as hunters carry, stated he was going "to Californy," and at sunrise started out toward the Northwest on a pathless journey which, to this strange man, was only a question of time and life; and he has not been heard of to this day.

Months afterward the Mexican guide of a scouting-party led the men, hungry, bewildered and nearly dead with thirst, to where he said there was, years before, a spring among the rocks. They found it, and near it a deserted "dug-out." From this to the spring was a well-worn path. When he saw it, the eyes of the professional "trailer" opened wide, but as he approached the hut, he threw up his hands with an astonished gesture, exclaiming, "*Madre de Dios,*—it was a woman!"

Upon the floor still lay the sodden fragment of a Spanish woman's "rebosa," and not far away the coyote-gnawed remains of a man's boot. What had become of the late residents, none could tell. But here at last was Jack's mystery; the house that he built, and in which Dolores and her last lover had met a fate which will never be known.

There have been men very like Othello, outside of Shakespeare. But Dolores was not Desdemona.

A HARVEST-DAY WITH THE PUEBLOS.

THE Pueblos are only Indians. But let not the reader imagine from this statement that he is again doomed to the description of the character, life, rights and wrongs, etc., etc., of the copper-colored Ishmaelite who, with no history of his own making, has entered so largely and so falsely into American literature. The Pueblo is included in the race only from a mistake made in the beginning and perpetuated through time. There is no distinction of race more perceptible than that which exists between him and the lawless freebooter who from time immemorial has been his enemy.

The long, low, grass-grown mounds which lie in the sequestered valleys and beside streams, in the remotest regions of New Mexico, are all that now remain to trace the outlines of those cities whose very names are forgotten, and whose last burgher died three hundred misty years ago. Those mementoes of a history upon which mankind can but speculate, and which is eternally lost, are the walls which protected the homes of the remote ancesters of the Indian farmers of the valley of the Rio Grande. The Pueblo is the small remainder in Northern America of the great people whose historic king and god was Montezuma, who founded the Mexican capital, who built the colossal temples of Central America, who had a written literature and a religion not utterly Pagan, and who, in the twelfth century of the Christian era, were as brave, as prosperous as and far less unscrupulous than the mailed adventurers from across the sea by whom they were conquered, and beneath whose rule they passed away as a people. You might not suspect it as you see him there in his humble village, engaged in patient toil in this bright harvest-time, but the Pueblo is the last of the Aztecs.

In contradistinction from the Indian, as we know the man usually meant by that term, the Pueblo is purely a farmer, and has been so from time immemorial. All his tastes and inclinations are peaceful. In his intimate knowledge of his business, his laborious patience, his industrious contentment in what the sunshine brings and the soil yields, he is the model farmer of America, and reminds one of all that has been said and written of the patient husbandmen of Egypt and China. It is astonishing to note how he is an unconscious teacher to those whose ancestors were his conquerors and oppressors. The whole curious routine of Mexican husbandry is borrowed from the Pueblo. His plough is made of two pieces of wood, the one mortised to the other at such an angle as makes at once the coulter and the beam. Sometimes, indeed, it is only the crotch of a tree, found suited to the purpose. Fastened to this are the long-horned, gaunt, patient oxen, yoked together by a straight piece of wood, bound with thongs to the horns. As one sees the brown-faced son of toil holding his rude plough by its one straight handle, walking beside the lengthening mark, which can scarcely be called a furrow, through the low field yet wet and shining from recent inundations, urging his beasts with grotesque cries and a long rod, one can hardly help thinking that the rude wood-cuts which illustrate Oriental agriculture in the Biblical commentaries have walked out of their pages, and are here before him.

And the Pueblo has modelled the universal architecture of the country. The low houses of sun-dried brick, with earthen roof, and earthen benches and beds and floors, had an origin far back of the conquest, and, though somewhat modified by it, are by no means the result of Spanish ideas of taste. But the Pueblo, a farmer by nature, had from time immemorial been surrounded by his enemy, the Apache. Therefore, the cluster of houses which formed the common village was each one a castle. The Pueblo made no doors, and when he and his family retired for the night, they climbed a ladder to the roof and drew the stairway after them.

A few villages are still the nuclei of a farming community, and the few inhabitants still, in the majority of instances, enter their houses through the roof. The orchards of peach and apricot, and the rich clusters of grapes, as well as the low-lying fields, are with immense pains, surrounded with an almost inaccessible wall. The Pueblo shuts in his life from the world and delights in isolation. His curious house and closely-fenced garden are not so from mere motives of fear. In common with all the aborigines of the continent, he seems bent upon isolation among the thousand changes which encroach upon him, and humbly passing away to join his fathers, without a memento, a monument or a word of history, save the meagre annals of his decline and death, told only by his conquerors. For three hundred years it has been so, and the picture presented seems an almost impossible one to the restless English mind. For centuries beyond which the poor Pueblo does not remember, with decreasing numbers, with new surroundings, with the predatory Apache and the covetous Spaniard, and latterly the Yankee stranger, ever peering over his garden wall, he has still toiled on, clinging to ancient habits, intensely occupied with the datails of the humblest of all lives, and most of all, content. Nor with all this would it be strange, if, as they tell, the light required by his ancient faith is still kept burning upon his hearth, and in his heart he still cherishes the faith that in the light of some radiant morning, the immortal Montezuma, high priest of the Sun, and king of the faithful, will come again from the east, bringing deliverence with him.

But it was the recollection of a harvest-day among the Pueblos that suggested all this. Far down the sandy valley as one approaches, stand the long lines of yellow walls, and far to the right glitter in the noon sunshine the slimy pools and yellow current of the musquito-haunted river. The settlement with the village for its centre, seems a large one. On every hand are the evidences of unwonted activity. The cumbrous carts, with framework of osier, howl dismally upon oilless axles, as they pass you on the roadside, to return freighted with yellow bundles. Here are four women, the oldest old indeed, and the youngest almost a child, who trudge along in the sand, each one's back loaded with fresh fruit. Did you ask for peaches? The eldest deliberately unloads herself by the roadside, opens her pack, selects a double-handful of the largest and ripest, and presents them with a smile upon her wrinkled old face. She will take no money, and trudges on, leaving you to look after and reflect that courtesy is not entirely confined to Christions with white faces. Perhaps the small incident is characteristic, for with just such kindness did this poor woman's ancestors welcome the strangers from across the sea, many centuries ago.

In the fields on either hand the reapers wade slowly

along, patiently decapitating each yellow stalk; and some distance ahead, a cloud of dust, and straw tossed high in air, and curious noises, proclaim the active operation of a primitive threshing-machine. Around a circular space some twenty feet in diameter, tall poles are set in the ground, and between these, from one to the other, are stretched strips of raw-hide. Within, the ground is bare and hard, and the newly-cut wheat, piled there, is being trodden out by some twenty unbridled donkeys. The small urchins kick and halloo in the straw outside the enclosure, like urchins in a straw-pile anywhere in the world, and two women and a man in the centre of the ring, so work upon the feelings of the asses with kicks and shouts, and sundry long poles, that they go fast and furious as Tam O'Shanter's witches' dance. To a man unaccustomed to close intimacy with the kind, there is ever something indescribably ludicrous in the long ears and solemn countenance of the genius *asinus*. Stir intense dignity and solemnity into friskiness, and the scene becomes absolutely laughable. As you watch these who tread out the corn on the ancient threshing-floor, you find yourself looking back as far as they are visible, intent upon seeing how with long ears laid backward, and flying heels, they revenge upon upon each other the thwacks of their masters.

Somehow, as you approach the village you gather the impression that all the women you meet are very large, and all the men proportionately lean and small. For aught I know it is a fallacy, but the average Pueblo woman is a creature whose brown comeliness and statuesque dignity might well challenge the envy of some of the queens of civilization. And you begin to discover that fruit is a specialty of these people. Laughing black eyes, whose owners' heads are just visible above the wall by the roadside, stand all a-row, and before each there is a huge melon and fruit-basket. This is the temporary market, instituted without any issue of bonds or previous arrangement, upon the arrival of every government train. I would there were some lone spot upon the habitable globe, where the tricks of traffic were unknown. Here, the fruit trade is rendered considerably more lively by the merry eyes, white teeth and brown and sturdy shoulders of a battalion of laughing market-women. Surely, the long train of wrongs which have pressed to the verge of extinction a hospitable and gallant race, have by these creatures been but seldom heard or poorly remembered.

The village has the appearance of being composed of blank walls. Only the square tops of the houses, and none of the domestic operations, can be seen. But the loaded boughs of trees droop over the walls, and here and there are glimpses of trailing vines and pleasant vistas. But it is in the midst of a dreary land, and the stretch of yellow grain-land between you and the cottonwoods of the bank, being rapidly divested of the burden of the summer, the suggestion of rest, quiet, contentment and plenty behind the drab walls, and the holiday faces around you, contrast pleasantly with the bold mountains which rise on either hand. In any more favored country, the simple pastoral scene which rests long with you in the hundreds of monotonous miles yet to come, might scarcely be remembered at all. From villages such as this, fenced about with walls upon one side of which grows the cactus by the straggling edge of the white highway winding away into distance, and upon the other verdure, and plenty, and content, the very name of this curious people is taken. "Pueblo" means only a town. The old name by which they call themselves, the name which expresses lineage and a country, I know not, and there are few who care.

Yet a little further, and there is another Oriental threshing-floor, upon which the scene is different from the last. The children and the revengeful donkeys have vanished together, and the hands and minds of the two stoical persons there are occupied in an operation so striking and important in the operations of simple life, that it was more frequently used as a simile than any other to teach the sons of the patriarchs the lessons which all men ought to know. It is the winnowing of the wheat. One of the persons is an old man, so withered of shank and so lean of face that he would seem to have been subjected to a process of drying for the sake of preservation. He stands by the rude fence, and anon with a small broom sweeps up each scattered grain as it falls beyond the heap. The other is a woman, and directly his opposite in all things. I cannot tell if it is always so, or if the picture I remember was only made for me, but I lingered and studied it. Surely, a woman winnowing wheat by the wayside is nothing. There could be no beauty or poetry there, and such things are the commonest incidents of common life. Yes, and we might see more in them if we would only look.

She was tall, and had a stolid and determined, but a most comely face. Her head was bound with a folded shawl, but her long hair escaped unconfined, and lay about her shoulders. Her outer garment was not a gown, but the dress of her race, so universally worn that it is a kind of uniform, being a large blanket of black wool, bound about the waist with a red sash. From the knee her limbs were bare, as were her arms and shoulders.

She stood with her left foot slightly advanced, and her great shapely arms held high above her head the broad saucer-shaped basket, over the edge of which poured the slow stream of mingled chaff and wheat. Considered merely as a bronze statue endowed with life, and without any reference to other endowments or qualities, this stalwart beauty who was utterly unconscious of herself, was the most perfect specimen of grace conceivable. When the padded queen of the ballet stands in the tableau, in an attitude meant to be the embodiment of gracefulness, but which is but a mincing and studied artificiality, then I know how very far any school of art is from what untaught nature attains, and think of the Pueblo squaw who winnowed wheat by the roadside in the July afternoon.

There was still another personage there, who at first escaped notice. His presence was not at all essential to the work in hand, but it would be a mistake to underestimate his personal importance. In the slant shadow of the straw-pile lay a big boy-baby, in the utter nakedness of nature. He tossed his brown round legs high in the air, in the lissome gymnastics of infancy, and while he gathered mysterious sustenance from the sucking of his left fist, with the other he clutched awkwardly at flies, straws, and the imaginary things which float in the air before the eyes of infancy.

It is a question whether the much-discussed question of "woman's rights" really had its origin in the minds of educated and progressive people. In all the aboriginal tribes of America, women have had their "rights," time whereof the memory of man runneth not to the contrary, and the truth is that these rights entail upon the sex as well in civilization as in savagery, that concomitant of equal drudgery which the Stantons and Logans would be very unwilling to assume. To all the privileges and labors of masculinity at least, the conditions of civilization are an eternal bar. Once, a robust Pueblo woman was selling *piñons* on the corner of the plaza at Albuquerque, and a sleek-looking infant lay on a blanket beside her. I got my chaperone to ask her how old the youngster was. She complacently answered, "day before yesterday," and pointed with her finger to that part of the sky where the moon was at that inconvenient hour in the early morning in which, I am credibly informed, babies everywhere are apt to come into the world. She was proud of the urchin, too, as all women are, and slipping her finger through his waistband held him dangling there like a human spider for our closer inspection. Such as these are alone physically competent to maintain rights.

So many strange stories are told and believed of the Pueblos—their religion, social customs and domestic life—that it is impossible to sift truth from falsehood. But they are the only one of the original races who have always been friendly to the white men. When General Kearney took possession of the Territory in 1850, in the name of the United States, the release from the peonage of many years so affected the hearts of these simple people that for a long time they clung to the belief that the commandant was the long-looked-for" man from the east," come for their deliverance. Repeated enforcements of this policy, and the final eradication of the evil; protection from Apaches, and general and reciprocal good treatment, have conspired to place this people in such relations with the great power destined before many years to absorb actually, as it now does in theory, the whole cen-

tral continent, as none others of the aborigines occupy.
It will not do to imagine that because the Pueblos are purely agricultural, they are incapable of defence. On the contrary, their whole history has been one of turmoil and strife. The Mexicans oppressed, and the Comanches and Apaches murdered; and these conflicts have been the direct cause of that air of ancient ruin and dead history which New Mexico wears. It is not the ancient and crumbling church, and the foot-worn and dilapidated village street, that are the oldest things in Mexico. Far back of the conquest existed the semi-civilization seen in the Pueblo village to-day. The cities whose walls are nearly imperceptible now, perhaps had bustling thoroughfares and a crowded population when the mound-builders of the Mississippi valley were at their strange work.

But these are questions for the savans. It is with the present, and with such things as are apparent in daily life, that this chapter has to do. We have said that through all these centuries of conflict and change, it was curious to note that manners and dress had remained so nearly unchanged. But that remark needs this further explanation, that it is of course impossible that contact with others should have absolutely no effect, and here is an instance. It is not missionary effort,—even the invincible phalanx of Jesuitism,—not Bibles, tracts or personal influence, which comes nearest the heart of the Pagan. It is cotton,—calico. The Indian of every tribe and latitude has obtained for himself a new character as the autocrat of the speckled shirt; and these people, with even a stronger individuality than his, are long since clothed upon with the new idea. Of all the girls, women, old men and children in sight, there is not one who does not wear it as the material of some curiously-cut gar--

ment. The old man who stands watching the winnowing, with the somewhat imbecile attempt at helping, has on only three separate articles of apparel, and two of them are cotton. Item, a pair of drawers, cut straight, wide and cool. Item, a shirt, made very much as that convenient article is throughout the world; and lastly, moccasons, whose broad soles retain the hair of the beast from whose skin they were made, and which turn over the toe in front. The statuesque woman wears beneath the black woollen uniform a snow-white garment, which conforms very nearly to the not unfamiliar pattern which, when worn alone, has the apparent merit of coolness, without any corresponding virtue as a covering. The girls who stand a-row behind the wall are all clad in the material whose familiar print takes one back at a bound to the square stone buildings which are the wealth and pride of the little Commonwealth of Rhode Island. But not as dresses are they worn, and it is only the *material* that is fashionable here, not the close-fitting, limb-confining devices with which the dames of a higher civilization torture themselves.

Here the idea of communism has been practically carried out for all these years. The village with its walls and gardens and curious houses has only a common purpose in its occupancy,—that of protection and society. There is no industry, except that connected with agriculture as the universal pursuit. There are no stores and no shops, and no sound of hammer or file. Every house was contrived for but two purposes,—residence and defence. There are not even streets, and only narrow paths wind among onion-beds and currant-bushes from one residence to the other. Each family is self-productive of every needed article of domestic economy, even to the fire-baked pottery from which they eat and drink. The black woollen garment was dyed after nature's recipe upon the back of the sheep, and the moccasons were contrived by the wearer. The clumsy cart, upon which the Mexican has been unable to improve, is cut and pinned and tied together by the unaided skill of the man who expects to use it. The only article of any constant use or importance, not actually made, is the cotton cloth heretofore mentioned.

Strangely enough, in all these things there is no diversity of style. Like birds' nests, as they are made now so they have been made from time immemorial. The porous earthern water-jug which hangs by cords from the rafters is of precisely the same material and shape in every house. The old idea of the biblical commentaries comes back again, when two women sit grinding at the mill, the loaf is baked upon the hearth, and the girls return from the spring, each with the tall water-jar upon her head. These people only need to live in dingy tents, surrounded by their goats and asses, and to be a little less heathenish in faith, to reproduce within the bounds of an overgrown republic, the days when Jacob worked for Laban, and was cheated at last, and the father of the patriarchs sat at his tent-door and watched the countless flocks which grazed in the future inheritance of his descendants.

And as the Pueblos produce all they need, so they are learned in all that it is needful for them to know. Long before the little monkish knowledge they may have acquired came to them from across the sea, they knew the times and seasons, and had a calendar in which the days of the year were three hundred and sixty-five. They practised then, as now, their patient agriculture with a-skill and success, some part of which would be a boon to farmers who subscribe for agricultural journals, and perchance have read Mr. Greeley's book. They knew how to take the metals from their native beds, and mould them into forms for ornament and use. Their brethren of the south built colossal piles of hewn stone. The fountains they made in thirsty lands are playing yet, and the trees they planted still cast their shade over the swarthy crowds which throng the streets of the Mexican Capital.

They have, indeed, through all these centuries gone backward and not forward. But the truth which is even now apparent, that for not one of all the aboriginal tribes of America is there any hope, will probably not be accepted as such until, within a few years, the end will have come. There is an isolation in the midst of surrounding life and activity which accepts no compromise with death. Ever the patient victim of change, and never the aggressor; with the material for a hundred histories, God only knows how heroic or pathetic, gone in the past; when the poor Pueblo shall finally leave his seed to be sown with a patent drill, and the harvest to be reapt by a clattering machine, he will merit at least the remembrance that his hands were never red with Saxon blood, and his hearth was abandoned without reprisal.

But before he goes, his eyes will see the white man's magic, in the engine rushing before its train down the valley of the Rio Grande, and the iron rail will usurp the place of the donkey-path in front of his door. And soon the denizens of whitewashed towns will have scared the husbandman from his plow, and the fruit-seller from the wall, and the noisy, civilized crowd will forget, if they ever knew, that in these regions there ever was so peaceful and pleasant a thing as a harvest-day with the Pueblos.

BROWN'S REVENGE.

OJO Caliente was of itself a prominent feature in a landscape bare and brown, and stretching in rocky monotony and silence for miles away on every hand. Even to people so learned that they claim in geology a sufficient explanation for all the strange things this world did when she was very young and soft, the decided freaks of nature are always invested with the terror of mystery and the charm of awe. As for this particular spot, many thoughtful eyes had looked upon it; many wise heads had speculated at its brink. A conical mound, very symetrical in shape and some thirty feet in height, rose from the surrounding plain. In its top was a circular basin about fifteen feet in diameter and of unknown depth, always full of limpid, sparkling, bubbling water. There alone in the thirsty land, the delicious element abounded, rejoiced and ran over. Clear, pure and—cold, of course? No, it was scalding hot. There was the feature; the mystery. It was one of those few mysterious openings into our common mother's fervid heart. Through a notch in the rocky basin's edge the pretty stream ran over, as large as a man's body; a volume which might have supplied a city with hot baths, and cleansed the grimy denizens of Constantinople itself. But it did not seethe and rage, and then compose itself in intervals of fitful and deceptive slumber. Through all' seasons and times, through heat and cold the stream was as constant as a woman's love, or—wickedness. Where the torrent spread itself out and cooled in the plain below, the tall weeds and coarse grass, and some hardy ferns grew rank and luxuriant, with their roots constantly bathed and warmed in a frost-defying bath. And the terrapins and wart-grown lizards, and long-legged and mottled toads, gathered there and lived a fortunate life. Amid the dense growth and balmy vapors, the rattlesnake forgot to stiffen his odious coils in a half year's slumber, and lay gorged and stupid, but still venomous, all the season through. The rough boulders gathered a green coat of slimy moss as they lay in the ooze, and in winter, when the hoar frost or the light snow lay on all the hills and plain around, that green acre lay in the slant sun like a bit of verdure strayed from the tropics.

Such a place, lying as it did on the main road from the low-country to the mountains, had not failed to attract attention and suggest a use. And that use was one which was of course in accord with the ideas and habits of the country. Ojo Caliente was a *ranche*, and while to a certainty the ranche idea could not be left out, it was also the result of a new idea in the wilderness; it was a watering place. The waters had medicinal properties, and an enterprising son of Old England occupied the slope of the hill with a rambling adobe, the front of which, standing next the travelled road, was the "store," while an array of rude chambers straggled up the slope toward the spring. Each was furnished with a long wooden tub, into which the water was conducted in a trough. Some tall cottonwoods flourished beside the wall, and gaining vigorous growth from the warm stream which touched their roots, gave an oasis charm to this one spot in the treeless landscape.

The place was likewise a hotel, and the smoke of a camp-fire arose each night from the trampled and dusty spot beside the garden, and mules brayed from the square enclosure which was supposed to be a sufficient protection from the Apaches. Here and there a limping rheumatic, or a sufferer from that insidious malady which is the just reward for an offense against God's great law of purity, sat and chafed his limbs and talked of his complaint and waited for health. Other than the waters there was no physician there. Neither was there any pretense of infirmity as an excuse for idleness and pleasure. Many a year must pass before fashion would here make illness an excuse for dissipation.

The proprietor of all this; the inventor and maker of all save the scalding spring, was a man whom every denizen of the country knew, and none knew well. He had come from they knew not where, and had prepared all these things with a lavish hand and no small expenditure of means. He was called rich, and daily adding to his wealth. His cattle grazed upon the surrounding hills, and with rare skill and vigilance, he kept them safe from the universal enemy. His place was known as a good place, and his meals were "square" meals. As neighbors go in that country he was a good neighbor, and many a mule was loaned, many a broken wheel mended, and many a meal given away, for men whom he had never seen before. Personally, he had failed to take upon him the likeness of the border. Middle-aged and gray-haired, he dressed in a civilized garb, and his oddly-shaven face had on it a look of settled unhappiness. To a stranger these things were seen and forgotten. "Odd feller," they said as they passed on, "wonder whar he come from," and that was all.

But those who knew him longer studied these peculiarities to better purpose. There was a rumor in the country that his name was not really Denham, and in

8

many a camp-fire talk it had been remarked that no man had ever heard him mention the place of his nativity, or speak of his family. We have called him an Englishman, but it was the unconquerable dialect of his youth which betrayed him. If conviction of crime depended only upon proof of nativity, no man could hope to escape, and many a man yet living in the Missouri River towns, could tell if he would, of the unfailing test of 1856.

And this was the only circumstance they could absolutely claim as knowledge. But no man ever questioned him, because, liking him well, there was something about him that forbade it.

He was proverbially quiet and even timid. He carried not the accustomed arsenal upon his belt, and was never known to take up a gun. In these things his hirelings acted for him, and while he had been known to stand calmly in his door and watch an Indian fight for the possession of his herds, the idea of assistance in the business seemed not to enter his mind. So, sometimes they called him "the preacher," and the baser sort nicknamed him "padre." And when by chance he heard them, he turned and walked away with a stricken look added to his habitual sadness.

Once, when a miner died at his house, and was filled with that late-coming penitence which usually comes lurking in death's shadow to punish the last hours of a hard life, Denham stood with others in the room. They told afterwards how "the preacher" seemed to restrain himself in the desire to perform accustomed acts. He came to the bedside and hastily went away again. Then he went out but presently returned bringing with him a small, worn volume, which he opened and essayed to read. The poor man's lips were dry and his face grew pale as he read, "I am the resurrection and the life; he that believeth in me"—and his voice choked in the utterance of the sublime words which take in all there is of hope, and he closed the book and left the place. More tutored men might have divined a truth in this, but they who remembered the scene only told it and wondered more and more at the man of mystery.

Frontiersmen are not inclined to love men who are not of their kind. But in this case after four years of divided opinion, the majority of the scattered residents who had aught to do with the proprietor of Ojo Caliente, were ready to fight for him. He did not swear, he refused to drink, he declined the use of slang. His language was such as some few of them could hardly understand, and with a retinue of female servants the suspicion of a single amour was out of the question. He counselled peace in the midst of strife. He gave advice to all who asked it, but meddled with the affairs of none. Each man thought in his heart that Denham regarded him as his best friend. He was acute and far-sighted, and a crowd of men ever ready to act more from impulse than reason, made a discovery of that fact. He was the repository of every bearded fellow's confidence in a radius of a hundred miles, and he kept their secrets like a priest. But they could not divest him of his strangeness. He read books, or, rather, a book. For a long time they thought it must be one some of them had heard of, mayhap seen,—the Bible. But when they had slily looked at the open page, they discovered that other scarcely less wonderful volume, Shakspeare. Once on a frosty night, when he broke in upon the story-teller's circle around the fire with a mild "listen a moment," having had a thrill of that wonderful "touch of nature" they clamored for more, and listened until the moon went down. And each rough son of the mountains carried ever after a bright imagining of she who would have borne the logs for Ferdinand, and fancied he could sometimes hear Ariel sing among the pines, as he delved for yellow dust.

Men who lead a strange life are generally unconscious of that life's peculiarities. Had his friends been critical they would have questioned the motives of a man who, while so unlike them, yet chose to live among them. With all his kindness, he was still a man apart. You could tell as he sat with thoughtful face at his door in the shimmering summer afternoon, that his heart was not in this country. He started at the slightest sound. He scrutinized strange faces with a kind of covert interest, and seemed ever ready to flee, abandoning all. The long-looked-for mail, which brought letters, evidently precious things to even the coarse and apparently hardened men around him, brought nothing to him. If Ojo Caliente and its lonesome landscape was not his home, then where could it be, since he had no interest in any other.

It is well known that the lonely graves of the border hide strange histories,—strange and untold. The boundless waste of plain and mountain is the great refuge of those who would hide from themselves. It is not the man doomed to spend the days of his years between granite walls; not him who sees his last goods go down under the sheriff's hammer; not even he to whom law is interpreted as the grim code which puts a halter upon his neck and his coffin beside him, who knows most of remorse, most of fear, and most of despair. Of all suffering men, he suffers most who, burdened with unknown and unpunished crimes, hides from the world. There is a punishment which comes at midnight, which no man can avoid. This is Hell. There is need of none more fiery. You think faces will tell the tale. No, there is no such incomparable liar as the human face. The man who scowls and frowns at the fit of a collar or the quality of a dinner, may live long and carry a gnawing devil in his bosom, and give no sign.

Thus, Denham ate and slept well, and looked after his affairs, and had only a melancholy face. But he was ever watching. As he sat at his door, and the evening shadows crept from distant mountains toward him, he could see the dim specks upon the yellow road which grew gradually larger and nearer, and they were not out of his sight or thoughts until nearness demonstrated their character and showed him their faces. This watchfulness was the man's visible sign of his trouble or crime, whatever that trouble or crime was. Not that his friends suspected as much. Watchfulness may be accounted for in a thousand ways, and is oftenest not regarded at all. Once convict, once suspect, and all signs are easily read and exaggerated by those whose faculty it is to hunt human nature down ; but the ordinarily careless eye may look for years and suspect nothing. And yet, there is ever more than natural oddity in the man who walks with bent head and locked hands, and upon whose ordinary occupations creeps constantly in the absent action, the muttered word, the startled look and the cat-like watchfulness of faces. The man Denham had these characteristics. "I rec'n, he's the feardest of Injins of any man in these parts," his neighbors sometimes remarked. Yes, he was afraid, but not of Indians. There was but one man of whom Denham stood in mortal fear, and he knew not if that one terrible creature were living or dead.

And in the long and tedious order of events which men may never control lest they should interrupt retribution, it came about that Denham's ghost came at last and sat himself down like Banquo at the feast. Even the far home in the wilderness is no refuge from fate. With grim pertinacity men's crimes, even their mistakes, hunt them out wherever they may go. One evening business, or a not uncommon desire to be alone, took him over the hill and far down by the sedgy slough. It may be that his brooding heart had that anticipation of evil which we imagine our inner consciousness sometimes has. But after an hour he returned slowly towards the house, his hands behind him, and his bent and prematurely-gray head regarding only his slow footsteps. Entering at the rear, he passed slowly through the low passage, pushing aside the canvass which hung as a door between each compartment. The frost of the late autumn of a prosperous year had come, and upon rude benches a half-dozen frontiersmen sat before the blazing fire in the public room, engaged in the old business of story-telling. He approached the strip of soiled canvass which hung between them and him, slowly as was his wont, and as he came, a voice which was not a familiar one, fell upon his ear. No, it was not familiar, for the man was a stranger, and yet,—what? Only this, that that coarse laugh was like a knell upon George Denham's senses, and his heart stopped as he sank upon a seat. Then, as he cautiously peered through upon the group he saw the stranger, lately arrived, full of talk, and the only man whose coming had ever escaped those watchful eyes. He was not a creature to be frightened at, only a bearded fellow of forty, red-faced and brawny-handed, as evidently a man whose best years had been spent upon the border as though the fact had been written upon him. Already he was on familiar terms with the men around him, and had begun the narration of his adventures. As Denham waited and listened behind the curtain, for confirmation of his fears, he knew the stranger did not lie as he talked.

"Gentle*men*," said he, "I never war here before, but I'm usen to this kind o'thing. I kim to Californy in 1850. I war young then, an I kinder struck a lead, an' havin' better luck'n most of 'em, I made money mighty fast. I stayed round thar fur twelve year,—yes, I recon it war that long, an' all the time,—*sartin* gentlemen,—I had a woman back in Injianny whar I come frum. That's a long time, you *bet*, an' finally I concluded I'd orter go back an' see my old gal,—a waitin' so long, you know. Well,—any gent as has a chaw o'terbacker kin accommodate *me*—as I wus a-sayin',—thank ye, boss,—I started fur to go back agin, an' when I got down to Saccermento, thinks I, what 'ud I be doin' fur to wag about forty thousan' miles wi' ten thousan' dollars in gold wi' me,—'cos that war jist what I had, an' might be a little more fur 'spences. Buy a draft, ses they. Draft, ses I,—we aint usen to no sich in my part o' the country. But the war wus broke out, ye know, an' I see some *mighty* purty bills,—they called 'em treas'ry notes,—as they said wuz as good as gold. Sez I, Mister, them 'll do, an' I chucked my dust inter ten o' the biggest. 'Twar a mighty small roll, I tell ye, fur to be worth ten thousand, an' I jest folded 'em into a slip o' paper an' chucked 'em into my jacket pocket an' started. It wuz carless, I know, but I 'lowed I needn't tell of 'em bein' thar. Well, I come clear across an' wuz 'most home, 'till I got on a railroad which I don't 'member the name, somewhar in Missoury. In the mornin', gentle*men*, when I felt fur it, *my money* *wuz gone!* It's been long ago now, an' all past an' gone, but I tell you, it *mighty* nigh got me. I wus a thinkin' of the old gal,—fact a dreamin' of her,—an' to wake up in the mornin' a sittin' in a seat a rattlin' to'rds home after twelve years' hard work, an' a poor man. Gentlemen, I aint much on the weakness, but I could a' cried. I tackled the conductor; ses he, thar aint no man got off this 'ere car sence you got on at one o'clock. Then he asked 'em, ses he, will any man object to bein' sarched, an' they sez no. Thar wuz no crack nor chink o' that car we didn't sarch. Thar wan't no man we didn't go through. Thar wuz no wimmin on, an' hadn't been, an' every last feller of the men wuz tickled fur to hev us to give 'em a sarch. Finally, sez the conductor, sez he, you haint never had it. I jest knocked him inter a old hat. I *wuz* riled, an' it wuz a comfort fur to do it. An' then I jest clim off that train an' started back. I haint seed my old woman. I *never* seed her—she's *dead*. Gentlemen, I'm a busted man,—I don't claim to be nuthin' else, *kin* you accommodate me pard?—thank ye.

As the speaker placed another quid in his mouth with indescribable gusto, there was a perceptible feeling in the circle of listeners. It is mistaken philosophy and mistaken religion, to speak of the 'hardness' of the human heart. It is careless and selfish, but there is no tenderer thing, when touched by that strain which defies all art and skill in its production, and which is like the unintended harmony we hear when the strings of a harp are touched by a baby's fingers or the trail of a passing robe. It was not intended, and a thousand attempts could not repeat it. But it was music nevertheless.

"But," said one who was younger than the rest, "why didn't you go home;—what did yer act thataway fur?"

Then the stranger turned his head slightly to one side, and closed his opposite eye, and regarded the speaker for a brief moment. It was the pantomime which means " What ails you?" or, in plainer terms " You are a fool."

"*Air* you aware young feller, that a man can't go home after twelve year, poor an' ragged an' ornery, an' tell 'em that he had ten thousan' dollars stole from him night afore last? Do ye think a feller's mother-in-law 'ud b'lieve any sich thing. Bah! that's too d—d thin." Then, as the young man retired into the shade of contempt, the speaker turned again to the circle of silent listeners, and continued. "Ye see, under sich circumstances a feller keeps his ragged britches on a purpus. He thinks he's a-goin' fur to hug his wife an' kiss his babies, an' be independenter 'n thunder, an' play it low down on 'em all fur about a week, an' then shell out the shiners an' buy a farm *d—d suddint;*—a feller kind o' wants to make the thing as *creamy* as possible, ye know. An' then to be busted *teetotal!* Them's hard lines, gentle*men;* I say them's d—d hard lines."

And all this time the man Denham sat unseen behind the narrow curtain and watched and listened. It was dark there, and only one lance of yellow light from the bright fire lay across his pale face. At first his countenance had a look of terror, and he glanced nervously about him, and felt his pocket, and looked into a far dark corner, where lay an old-fashioned portable expressman's safe, probably purchased at some quartermaster's auction sale. Then, as the talk went on, his look changed, his mood melted, and the dim shadow of a great resolve came into his eyes. But nobody can describe the emotional panorama which a man's face is popularly supposed to present under such circumstances, because if these changes occur at all, it is only when the restraint of other eyes is taken away. We have already said, with this man Denham for an example, that men's faces are always liars. But a change came over him as he listened, whether perceptible or not. He arose silently and went on tiptoe to the safe which lay in the corner. He felt in his pocket for a key, and very quietly and cautiously took from it a packet, seeming to be a folded written document of some length. Then he went quietly back and seated himself until the stranger's story was ended.

They were "hard lines" he had said, and almost as he uttered the words, Denham came among the group. He did not sit down, but where the light fell full upon his face stood regarding the stranger. "Do you know me?" he asked calmly.

"W'y,—well, no,—not adzactly. How'd do?" And the good fellow rose and proffered his hand with a look of inquiry and anticipation.

Denham feigned not to see the hand which it seemed he dare not take, and the stranger seated himself again. He stood looking at the fire in forced calmness, but his eyes were blood-shot and his voice hoarse. Presently, as by a mighty effort, he said:

"Friends, I have something to say to this man William Brown,"—the stranger started—" and to you all. Please, listen to me, and remember that I now appoint you all to be my judges and my jury. Some of you tried and hung the horse-thief at Pinos Altos, and two of you captured and brought back the man who killed Tom Hicks, and he was tried and shot. I am ready to stand by your verdict. God knows I want no better men."

The bronzed and bearded group upon whom the firelight glanced as this man seemed to place his life in

their hands, sat silent. It may not have seemed as
strange to them as it does to the reader. They were the
law-makers, as well as the executors, of the country in
which they lived. No cringing prayers, no promises, no
tears availed with them. Yet, the American history,
which is yet to be written, will not deny justice to the
grim law-makers of the border. Every man's life was
in his brother's hands. They dealt justly, not as under
the abstract obligations of a juror's oath, but as each man
himself hoped for justice.

Perhaps they did not understand the speaker's words
precisely, but they sat unmoved and waited. It was not
a mercurial court; they would see it all by and by. The
speaker continued. "William Brown, I heard your
story, and I know and declare to these men that it is
true. See here," and he held up in his hand a small
square volume; "this is a Bible. I believe this book to
be God's book, and hereon I solemnly swear that *I am
the man that robbed you!*"

Another tremor went round the circle, but no man
spoke. Only the stranger rose up. Some who read this
may imagine the ease with which a man handles a long-
used tool. Some may know how the soldier tips his
musket, or the flash-like movement in which the Lascar
slips his crooked knife from its greasy scabbard into the
bowels of his antagonist. Such as this, is the intimacy
of the borderer with his terrible weapon. Ere he could
speak again, or scarcely think, the slender muzzle of
Brown's pistol was in the criminal's very face.

But there were other quick eyes and hands there, and
as the avenger hesitated a moment to speak, old Joe
Maxwell's hand was upon his arm. "Sit down, stranger,"
he said, "*we're* a tryin' this, an' don't want no interferin',"

and he looked out of his gray eye a glance which meant much more than he said.

In the sense of a lofty purpose, Denham grew courageous, and in the silence that ensued he took from his pocket the packet and unfolded it, and handed it to old Maxwell. "Can you read it?" said he. The old frontiersman looked doubtfully at it, handed it back and remarked, "read it yourself, an' I rec'n we'll git the sense on it."

"Gentlemen," said Denham, "this is my will and my story together. I wrote it a year ago, for a man may die, and though I never thought of showing it in my lifetime, I am glad of the opportunity, because I can remedy my crime, die easier, and be thought better of after I am dead. As between this man and me, I have suffered most, and justly. I could tell my story, but this explains it all and in less time."

His auditors probably did not know it, but as the criminal stood close by the guttering candle, with the light of duty in his face, he looked a clergyman at a funeral. His manner, forgetting himself, was that of a man once accustomed to such duties. He opened the paper, and solemnly read what is here set down:

"IN THE NAME OF GOD, AMEN. I, James Dodd, clergyman of the Church of England, of Witham, in the County of Essex, and now of the United States of America, do herein write my last WILL and TESTAMENT, and do hereby enjoin that it shall be executed, though without witnesses and wanting legal form, for I would that I might die without shame, and that none should read until I am dead."

"I give unto one William Brown, once of the State of Indiana, and now of parts unknown, and unto his heirs and assigns, my property of Ojo Caliente, and all lands, houses, appurtenances and fixtures thereunto belonging. And I give unto him and them my strong box, and all therein, namely, twenty-three thousand dollars in coin and dust. I give unto him and them all my cattle and goods, and all property of all kinds, to have, hold and use the same forever."

"And I hereby enjoin upon all to whom this shall come when I am dead, that they by no means interfere with the injunctions of this my Testament, for I declare that what I give to the said William Brown and his heirs, is already theirs, of which truth to the doubting I commend the following, my confession :"

"I am sixty-two years of age. I came to America in the year 1848, and was born in the County of Essex, in England. I was a clergyman, and all my life until the time whereof I speak, I have feared God, and praying always, walked in His law. If, by mercy, they yet live, I have a wife and two daughters, whereof the eldest must now be twenty years old. More of them I will not tell, for since the time whereof I shall speak, they have not seen my face, and I would that they and I should suffer all manner of apprehension and sorrow, and that they should think me unfortunately but honorably dead, than know of my sin and crime."

"I was poor, and though I urge not this as an excuse, God knows the longing of a man for his family's sake. I thought often of how I should improve my condition, and dreamed of wealth. Yet, could not I attain it. I dare not abandon a calling for which God and not my flock, knew how little I was fitted, for it secured my bread. Thinking these thoughts, I was on a railroad train in the state of Missouri, on the night of December 22d, 1862.

On the car were only eleven persons, males, for it was a bitter night. I arose and stood near the stove, and a lamp burned dimly above my head. And as I stood there there came a rough man, and standing beneath the light, and seemingly careless of my presence, he took from the pocket of his vest a small flat package, folded tightly in a piece of yellow paper, upon which was a name. He unfolded the same, and as I looked he counted certain bank-notes, called as I knew Treasury notes. They were new, and at first I looked from curiosity. I perceived there were ten of them, and that each was of the denomination of one thousand dollars.

I went again to my seat, and the man to his. But I pondered of the money I had seen. In my heart I thought that God had not been just to me. The man, I saw, was a rough and uneducated man, and he, I thought, will spend this all in the pleasures of such as he, while I, knowing so much of what money may bring, am deprived of all."

"And I thought further. How, said I, might a man obtain this money and go happy and unpunished. I knew that criminals were fools, but I thought I could do better than a common thief. Where should I hide it that I might calmly defy search? I arose and went near the man, and I saw that one small corner of the package was above his pocket. My face burned; I could feel the blood racing in my veins. So near it seemed, so easy. I went again and looked into my small travelling-bag. There was no hiding-place there, for men look keenly into linings and corners wherever they may be, and there is where mere thieves make mistakes. But I unconsciously took into my hand the commonest article in life, a cake of soap,—only a small square, new and unused.

I carried this with me into a place of concealment and locked the door. I cut from the end a small mortise, and carefully saved the piece. Then I hollowed out the interior,—not too much,—and saved the crumbs. I remember as I looked upon this simple and childish piece of work, that it was indeed an infernal machine. But I again approached the sleeping man, snoring heavily upright in his seat. I looked around; there was not a wakeful person in the car. As I gently drew out the package, and knew that I held ten thousand dollars in my hands, my hair rose upon my head, and *crime, crime, crime,* seemed to ring in my ears. But it seemed too late to go back. Half wild, I retreated, and in a few seconds the money was sealed in the soap-cake, the end which had been cut slightly bruised upon the floor, as if by falling, and the whole was in my bag and I in my seat."

"Very soon, it seemed to me, the man awoke, and in a moment called out that he had been robbed. The doors were locked, the train stopped, and every man offered himself to search. Hats were turned out, valises emptied and every nook investigated. I offered mine with avidity. Having yielded to crime I became hardened. The cake of soap fell on the floor, a man picked it up, mechanically smelled of it, handed it to another, and finally it was tossed upon a seat and left for many minutes."

"Finally, it became apparent that there were no thieves on that car, and a general impression prevailed that the man had lost no money. But when the train-conductor told him as much, and blamed him for causing the loss of time, he was stricken down by a brawny blow, and the cruelly robbed and wronged man left the train and went out into the bitter night, raving and cursing, utterly ruined."

"But as the train sped on its way, there was one even more wretched than he. I was afraid of my shadow. I dared not return to my honest wife and my prattling children, and account for my wealth. Since then I have not seen them, nay, nor any creature who could remind me of my days of purity. I have been punished, for I would give my life to even hear of those toward whom I dare not even look."

The reader ceased, and raising his eyes and hands, exclaimed, " and now, may God through Christ, mercifully forgive all my sins, and restore to this man his own, and let me die."

There was a deep silence. The stranger had turned from red to pale, and sat gazing motionless into the fire wrapped in thought. Years had quenched the bitterness of his wrong, and as he looked at the man who had suffered more than he, he seemed to forget vengeance. Finally, old Maxwell rose, hitched up his waistband, drew his hand across his eyes, and said : " This *are* bad, but 'taint no *killin'* offense in my opinion," and sat down. But his words elicited no response. The group sat silent, looking into the dying fire, their heads bent, and each man evidently thinking more of the strangeness of the story than of his function as juryman. Finally, the stranger arose slowly, buttoned his ragged coat, looked around him upon the group, and advanced slowly toward Denham.

"Parson," said he, "I told ye all I wuz busted. I haint got no luck. My gal's dead, an my friends is forsook me. *You* done it,—done it sneakinly on a sleepin' man. I don't want nothin' *now*,—I don't want yer orspital, or yer bilin' spring, or yer gold. You kin burn yer will,—ye kin keep yer curse, an' I'd even scorn to kill ye. Let me tell ye something which, with all yer smartness ye aint learned yit. Ye can't cure the blight of a man's youth by *givin' back!* *I* haint no children,— no wife,—no home,—no character,—no nothin', an' ye can't *give* them things to me. I tell ye, I'm busted, an' *you* done it. Parson! fool! thief!—I want none of yer trumpery, keep 'em an' be damned eternally to you."

And hurling this frightful anathema behind him, he strode through the door and out into the night, and his footsteps died away upon the road.

One by one the rough men arose, and silently, and with no glance aside, went away, and James Dodd, clergyman and thief, was alone in his stolen house and with his stolen wealth.

They spent no time in parleying; they wrote no sentence, but the verdict was, to be forsaken and despised in the loneliness of disgrace and crime.

And when the frosty sunlight streamed through the dusty panes in the early morning, the face it shone upon was a dead man's waxen mask, and the suicide had ended all, with one ghastly gash from ear to ear.

The spring murmurs on, and the tall cottonwoods grow green and beautiful in the desert. Nature and truth alone are triumphant, for the ranche has crumbled into decay, and the fair church of Saint Lazarus was built with the stolen gold.

A DAY WITH THE PADRES.*

THAT lonely and far-away tract of wilderness which became ours through that contest which made General Taylor a hero and a president, whose Capital, the "City of the Holy Faith," was occupied first by our army in 1850, and which from that time has been called, in contradistinction from the immense domain from which it was wrung, New Mexico, has been the victim of all the governmental vicissitudes which are the common inheritance of foster-children. In its legislative chambers, the same rancorous oratory is indulged in; the same voluminous and useless statutes are enacted, repealed and amended; the same caucusses and conspiracies are held; the same private interests are looked after in the name of the public good, as in our own virtuous Commonwealth, or any other of the glorious thirty-seven. In some of these things New Mexico has gone beyond her sisters, and her senate chamber has been the arena in which murderous hate has ended in blood, and beside its Speaker's chair, men have died by the bullet. Only one thing she yet lacks. Be patient, statesmen. The day will come when, clothed in uprightness and throned in honor, her legislature will be called upon to elect senators.

Then, at every change in the administration, and sometimes oftener, comes the more or less obscure man, a stranger to the people and their habits and interests,

---

* This chapter was not written in the interests of any religious controversy,—with which the author in these pages has nothing to do,—but simply as a narration of facts apparent to any observing resident, regardless of religious bias.

often incompetent from the beginning, and always embarrassed by his new surroundings, who for a brief period is to be Governor of the Territory. Included in his dominion, is that wild and remorseless scourge of civilization, the Apache, and the swarthy, power-loving Spaniard, the traditions of whose race, and whose national instincts, almost forbid a conception of that form of government which he has cause sometimes to consider unjust, which he privately regards as an experiment, and which in his heart he dislikes. For a brief time, this man holds in his hands the power which is nominal, and wears upon his unaccustomed brow the laurels which of all green things fade soonest; and another, better or worse as chance shall decide, but uniformly the average politician, comes to take his place—but always to sit in the same uneasy seat, to enjoy the same transient honor, and to retire in the same disgust.

But this yearly legislature, this periodical governor, and this roster of secretaries and judges, are not the rulers of New Mexico. They do not control its affairs, or prescribe its code, or occupy any place in the hearts of its people. Who is the ruler? You need hardly turn your eyes aside to see him. You need not crowd any ante-chamber or attend any levee to catch a glimpse of him. He has no mansion, holds no receptions, makes no appointments to office, and places his distinguished autograph upon no legislative enactment. He has no wife, and no children that are called by his name, nor any social relations. The President of the United States may send as many governors as he pleases, the legislature may manufacture statutes at its august pleasure; when they have done all, this man alone has power, and he alone rules. You may see this actual governor any day upon the village street. His long black coat floats behind him as he passes by. His step is soft and his demeanor humble, and his broad-brimmed hat sits squarely over a downcast eye and a pale and smoothly-shaven visage. As you look at him you know he is one who has no vices, and is a man of midnight devotions, of long vigils, and of fasting and prayer. An odor of sanctity lingers in his path as he hurries by. Sturdy, rebellious, fighting Puritan though you may be, you somehow feel that your steady stare as he passes you had better have been a humbler one, and that the reverent upward glance, the hurried sign of the cross and the whispered *benedicite* you might have had for the asking, would do you no harm. Of all the hundreds with whom he associates and whom he influences in this strange country, this man is the only one who thoroughly understands himself and has a definite purpose in living. With all others the purposes and ambitions of life change with years and circumstances. He has no dreams, and is not disturbed by ambition. He has devoted himself to a purpose, which in all the annals of the remarkable brotherhood to which he belongs, none of his kind have ever been known to abandon. The footsteps of his successors have been marked with privations, hunger, toil and the flames and tortures of triumphant martyrdom. If this man were called, he would follow in their footsteps. In short, this humble governor of the people is a member of the Society of Jesus. The heroism of his brethren is historic, and in all that we may say of him, let us begin by being just. To the mother-church he is son, brother and husband, and to him she is wife, mother and sister. He brought his faith, his zeal and his unscrupulousness with him when he came across the sea with the mailed and dauntless adventurers of Spain three hundred years ago. Wherever they bore the sword, he carried the cross; and with an inconsistency which is not the least curious fact in the history of the great church, he proclaimed the religion of the meek and lowly One amid the smoking signs of rapine, desolation and unjustifiable conquest. The diamonds and gold and life-waters he sought were in the hearts of men; and when the soldier had departed the Jesuit stayed. Amid all the changes of three centuries he has remained. His depleted ranks have been constantly recruited. An adventurous explorer, carrying his influence and his faith into wilds so remote and so inhospitable that he never returned; working, enduring, scheming, moulding, through all these ages he has never forgotten his Master or his Order.

In view of all this, there is nothing wonderful in the fact that New Mexico is one of the most thoroughly Catholic countries. In all these barren hills and silent valleys the foundations of this mightiest of all the fabrics reared in the name of Christ are deep and strong. To these people the church is a passion, strong as it is among the Andalusian hills. In this one spot alone, in broad, free-thinking America, can be found the church of Saint Peter as it is, and is intended to be. Not in Rome itself, are its essential features more perfectly preserved. The pomp and circumstance and imagery, the elaborate ceremonial and intricate form, the gloomy and awe-inspiring mystery, and the blind and dumb belief,—are all there. The religious, or rather the church idea, pervades all the classes and conditions of life. Beginning at Santa Fe the names of nearly all the towns are suggestive of saints, or crosses, or passions, or sorrows. The boys are frequently named Jesus, and the daughters some one of the

Queen of Heaven's countless designations. The emblem of the cross is everywhere, and the old and crumbling church which stands in the plaza, as most of them have stood while the generations have been gathered around them in slumber, are the centres of all life, and the neuclei around which cluster all there is of society, interest or affection.

These church buildings themselves are evidences of the modifications of which Catholicism is capable, in adapting itself to ignorance. There is one system for the refined and educated, and (with its essential ceremonies unchanged) quite a different one for the credulous and unlettered. The walls are hung round with the commonest of colored prints of saints, angels, crucifixions and flaming hearts. The altar blazes with candles, and brass, and crimson calico, and there is a wooden railing in front, beyond which the most daring of curious worshippers never ventures. But the costly and ornate surroundings with which the Romish church is wont to aid her worship, are unattainable on this far verge of Christendom. Within these mildewed walls the mighty diapason and the thrilling voice-like tenor of the old world organ have never sounded. In the rude gallery, the musicians who answer feebly to the priest's responses are the same, with the same instruments, who furnished the thin strains at last night's fandango. But never is the ceremonial wanting in that mystery and solemnity by which the simple hearts which deem this grandeur are impressed. Tawdry and cheap as the surroundings are, all the instruments of ancient power are still present. The touch which is holy, the genuflection which is saving, the words which bind or loose on earth or in heaven, are never absent. When the book is closed, and the bell is rung, and the candles are extinguished, the pall which falls upon the excommunicated soul is as terrible in its darkness, and as frightful in its doom, as though launched at the sinner from the high altar of Saint Peter's. In many instances the building is holy from its very age. Here, the Mexican peasant reflects, worshipped his father and his grandfather, and within its sacred precincts their bones are mouldering. The earthen floor has been hardened by the pious knees of those for whose souls' repose he prays. Bodily and visibly sacred to him, he deems the legend carved above the door to be very truth when it tells him, "This is the gate of Heaven." And over all, the guardian of his inheritance, the agent of his soul, presides his silent, amiable, sad-faced pastor, learned in those things which it is not for such as he to know, and versed in the mysteries of that fated book which he dare not read. Obedience to this man is his only hope. He is clad in a mysterious power. He is learned, he is silent, and with the common things of life he has naught to do. The wily, patient Jesuit seems to him to lead a higher life, and to be clothed with mystery. And when he comes to die, no lips but the padre's can whisper in his ear those words which his soul must carry with it as the Shibboleth which opens the crystal gates. It is he who in this world prescribes the doleful penance for unwonted sins, and whose prayers shorten the term of punishment hereafter. He it is who knows the inmost secrets of a sinful life, but whose lips are sealed by an almost supernatural power. Through the confessional, earth and heaven are both in his hands. In truth, this man is the governor of the country.

In these matters I would not wrong the priest. In the doing of these things he follows as blindly as he leads.

For the deceptions he knowingly practises upon his flock, he claims the excuse of necessity; but he too must wash his soul by vigils and prayers, and his lips also must find absolving touch, or he is lost. A power which he reverences even as the peasant reverences his, enjoins many a midnight vigil and many a hard penance. And so onward through all the grades of sacerdotal authority until at last it touches the chair of Saint Peter, and ends in infallibility itself, impersonated in the poor old man who wanders in the corridors of the Vatican, tortured by the encroachments of the temporal power, and wondering that the crowns that once waited for his setting, now mock the tiara upon his own gray head.

The church in New Mexico is always open. But early each morning the sleeper is awakened by the ringing of the bells which call to matins. Then the senoras hurry along the streets; the peasant leaves his fruit-basket or his donkey-load of wood; and each, casting worldly cares aside, enters the rude doorway bent upon duty. Each stops at the dilapidated barrel at the door which contains the holy water, reverently besprinkles himself, bows toward the altar and falls upon his knees, busily muttering the prayers of whose meaning he has small conception and whose repetition is a matter of merit rather than feeling. As for the senorita, she draws near the altar and occupies the choice places of the sanctuary, but the fruit-vender and the fuel-merchant, clad in the coarse garments of poverty, creep far into a corner and pray from afar off. Within the altar-rail, stands the priest, muttering in a monotone, as if for himself alone, the prayers which seem to be an unpleasant monotony. A single acolyte, being a prematurely-awakened and rather sleepy lad, swings a censer beside him. Compared with the awakening hum of the dewy morning without, the scene seems dreary enough. The braying of asses, the cackling of domestic fowls, and the bleating of flocks are heard. Perhaps the dreary roar of the sunrise gun from some neighboring fort breaks in upon the prayer; or the regular cadence of a passing squad of guards wakes echoes strangely at variance with holiness. The hasty services are soon over, and the worshippers whose consciences pricked them into attendance go forth again more gladly than they came. But the old church still stands with its wide-open doors, and he who will may come and pray. So it will stand, and its morning and evening bells will jangle, for a dull century yet to come.

But where you have stood thus far is not *the church;* and if you are a stranger and an American, and possess some of the true *gringo* impudence, you may conciliate the padre, and he will show you all those things whereby this sketch was suggested.

First of all you may notice the curious wooden boxes, with doors in front, very much after the fashion of a wardrobe. The padre smiles and passes on as you stop to regard them. He knows that in your Protestant ignorance you have never poured your miserable tale of secret crime, through a piece of perforated tin, into the ear of a listening priest. He divines that you need no explanation, for those are the confessionals. Here, you see the actual means by which the church gains over her children the rule of fear. God knows how many murderous dagger-stabs, with all their villanous motives and rewards, have been detailed in whispers at that box. You imagine as you stand there, the story of the frail woman a hundred times repeated, pardoned by virtue of confession only to sin again; and you wonder as you watch the black receding figure, if that priestly coat really conceals a heart burdened with the knowledge of countless crimes, the mere whisper of which would turn to hate the loves of years, and build scaffolds, and sharpen daggers, and make demons of placid men and fiends of careless women.

Upon a rude wooden frame below the altar, the most prominent feature in the body of the church, stands a figure so curious in its appearance, so uncouth and tawdry, that you wonder to think that this babyish image represents the central figure in all the worship of the mother-church. It is a wooden doll, three feet high, whose features approach no more nearly to womanly, or even human, beauty than do the rude caricatures of school-children. Upon the head is a gilt pasteboard crown, and at the feet are artificial roses. The awkward wooden fingers are encased in cotton gloves. A pink gown, a long veil, gaudy knots of ribbon and gay finery complete the figure. It is hideous. You hardly deem it possible that such a thing could answer any religious purpose. Nevertheless, before this image none pass erect and with covered head. Before it are offered the sinner's humblest prayers and costliest gifts. This is she to whom the sorrowing hearts of millions turn for hope and comfort. It is the Queen of Saints, the Mother of Sorrows, the Star of the Sea, the Mother of God. Before this monstrous thing, every day, and almost every hour, heads are bowed to the very earth, and to it are fervently offered the longest prayers the worshippers know.

But with a look upon his face which seems a reproach, the padre waits for you at the door of what may be termed the property-room of the church. Here you perceive, on all hands, the odds and ends of sanctity. There are the long wooden sticks painted white, which, with a taper in the end, do duty as wax candles in many processions. In one corner stands an image which, having met with an accident damaging to some of its prominent features, is laid up for repairs. There are branching candlesticks, canopies, croziers, banners and vestments. Upon one side of the room, in ancient drawers, are quantities of linen, and vestments of scarlet and lace. You cannot touch them; you may just peep and pass on. Here is a long wooden box, in size and shape very suggestive of the cemetery. What does it contain? You are answered whisperingly that within it is kept a life-size image of Christ. Surely that is enough, and you have no further curiosity. There are relics there too, you are told, such as few churches possess, and baptismal and marriage records so old that the parchment is in rags. But you are glad to pass out into the sunshine, and get away from a place where people who worship the same God and believe in the same hereafter you do, should teach you such strange religious experiences.

Outside, the graves lie so thick that there seems to have been a contest for occupancy. And such is really the case. The skulls of ousted occupants grin at you unburied. The ground is sacred, and the church derives a revenue from the sale of graves. Therefore, the whole place has been dug over and over again until it is a Golgotha.

And now, as you depart, it is well to remember that among all these things, not the least curious is the padre himself. He well knows how you and all your kind regard those things he has had the courtesy to show you. He could probably see your thoughts in your face. But he has made no sign, offered no argument, and only endeavored to gratify your curiosity and do you a service.

He leaves you at the door with a courteous gesture and a smile, and you go as you came, unquestioned, and he turns back again to his life's purpose. True to his character in all things, your Jesuit is also a gentleman. You may smile or be shocked at his faith and his worship, you may hate his teachings and his Order, but he will force you to remember one good among the evil,—the courtesy of a stranger.

So numerous are the *festas*, or holy days, that long before the year is ended two-thirds of it seems to have gone in processions in honor of innumerable saints. What of religion there may be in the motley and irregular processions which ramble through the streets, hooting, screaming, and firing ancient and rusty blunderbusses loaded to the muzzle, is apparent only to the Mexican mind. In them there is no solemnity, and not a shadow of anything like devotion. Sometimes two irate devotees stop and engage in the manly art, and frequently the bearer of an image to which he has often prayed, puts down the wooden saint while he indulges in a draught of *aguardiente*. These occasions are the laughter and sport of the whole *gringo* population, and their efforts in evoking fun out of the occasion are often a source of serious inconvenience in the performance of the noisy rites. In the Capital city there has been resident for many years a half-idiot, who has always been the available man to impersonate Christ on the cross, in an annual festival in which that representation is necessary. Certain evil-disposed heretics informed the fellow that if, every time the procession passed a certain spot on the plaza, he would come down, they would give him a drink of that fluid which he dearly loved. His mind was not so much impaired that he was likely to forget so precious a promise as that, and when the procession came to the spot, the miserable impersonation of the victim of the most fateful tragedy the world ever saw so struggled and screamed in his awful position that he was taken down and permitted to indulge his appetite. The scene occurred again and again, and the scandalized padres and their flocks had only the alternative to abandon, or endure. Those whose cheeks burn as they read this recital of a scene to which there are yet living witnesses, need no further explanation of the atrocious mummeries of these religious processions.

The true church life here is one long penitence in the way of expiating the sins of the soul by the sufferings of the body. Such of necessity is the case in a land whose people are so deeply and constantly stained with social crime. One man goes for a prescribed period with small stones in his shoe; another wears round his waist a knotted thong; a third eats no meat; etc., etc. But these are the lighter punishments; there are others which are severe even to cruelty. There is an organization known as the "Flagellants," who lash their bare backs with stinging cactus, and as the blood trickles from the cruel stripes, they gather satisfaction from the reflection that the excess of punishment over what is necessary to atone for their own sins, stands to the credit of the Catholic world in general. Some of the penances partake largely of the ridiculous, such as sleeping in the church-yard, and knocking the head upon the church-steps. It seems that the fragile senoritas get off very nearly free, and are mainly required to say an unwonted number of prayers, or confine themselves to a less number of lovers; either of which would prove something of a cross to them. It is strange that with the knowledge of the crime and the means of punishment both at hand, the spiritual agent of these erring souls accomplishes nothing further in checking the crying sin of society and the race. But in the midst of janging bells and constant prayers, through confessions and penances and rituals, one of the most thoroughly Catholic, not to say religious, countries in the world, is debauched to its very core. The fact stands unchallenged that female purity is unknown. Only the dagger or the bullet checks the course of illicit love. The fearful things that follow in its course pass on and on in an endlessness whose ghastliness defies even pity. And in this sacerdotal devil-fish, whose tentacles grasp the very hearts of the people, there is no hope. With a foundation laid deep in ignorance and superstition, it has held them for nearly three hundred years, but has held them for the church, and not for truth. The unknown graves of all its martyrs in the wilderness are the graves of the martyrs of a church, and not of a religion; and the end will not be until men own the souls for which they are accountable.

Truly, as I remember him, the padre seems the pervading spirit of every dreamy Mexican day. The placid street would want its character if I failed to recall him as he flitted silently by. I could scarcely recall the sunshine's yellow glow across the hills, were it not for his intervening shadow. The stalwart Pueblo woman, gentlest and most deeply wronged of all the aborigines, smiles pleasantly as she unrolls from his blanket her big naked baby for you to see, and lo! the priest is there. You watch the swarthy, noisy little boys as they play at bull-fight by the garden-wall; and even as you wonder to think that in all times and races the children are the same, comes the padre with his stick, the fun is over, and he and they are gone together. If you stand and watch the still evening fade into still calmer night, while the Tyrian dies grow gray above the pines, and the bold hills seem to wrap themselves in an inky cloak; even then, a black-stoled figure glides between you and the fading light, and you lose the sense and scene in wondering at his ubiquity. Every idle hour and trifling scene which is present with me in my recollections of that dreamy land, finding a place in thought by virtue of some hidden charm, seems brooded over by this same Jesuit. And as I think of him, I recall all that others have told of him and his influences, in the still older land where he and his sombre brood were born: the days when Spain was the incubus of Europe; when Philip brooded in his cell in the Escurial; when the Inquisition held its horrible sittings; when Coligny was murdered in his bed, and Navarre of the white plume was stabbed in the street; aye, when the red vision of the exile of Patmos brooded over all the crowns and thrones of Europe, as she broods today over the barren hills and sombre valleys and squalid villages of New Mexico. This is the day of his possession; the time of his strife is yet to come. The horde which wanders toward him is a horde of Vandals and iconoclasts. The small white churches, whose pastors are the bright sons alike of Democracy and Protestantism, will yet nestle among the hills, and these vivacious children will yet whoop and halloo and chatter in the English tongue. Yes, but then the subtle charm will have departed; the peace of contentment and ignorance will have forever flown. When the charm which clings with the ivy to dilapidated things is gone, and the land is redolent of pine and paint and energy, then will have been washed out, not without its memories and regrets, the last footprint of the old world upon the new.

JOE'S POCKET.

"DRUNK ag'in, I sw'ar. Joe Biggs, you *air* the orneryest human as lives. Drat yer, say nuthin' to *me*, fur I can't stand it. *Thar's* the bed." And the maligned Joe Biggs blindly flung himself upon the creaking cords of a not-very-luxurious couch, aided thereto by a movement on the part of the speaker which was too sudden to be regarded as a caress.

The people outside laughed a little as they heard this berating, and began a hasty retreat as the tumbled flaxen head of the woman immediately after appeared at the doorway. Moonlight is kind to beauty, but homeliness, as embodied in a face fairly chalky in unhealthy whiteness, a hay-colored mass of unkempt hair, a scowl which boded no kindness, and over all a shabby night-dress, has no friend in the beams which seem to cover all except such deformities as these. The woman turned away again and retired into the darkness of the shanty, the retreating footsteps of the roysterers died away in the distance, and soon, under the placid light, it was as though there were no drunken men or cross women in all the world.

It was a cabin by the side of a mountain road. The huge pine logs of which it was constructed had been cut from the stumps hard by; and so far as rude skill and main strength could make it so, the place was comfortable enough. It was the ancient pattern of the "cabin." There was one door and one window, a chimney of mud and stones, and a small yard was enclosed with an apology for a fence. It was the hill-country, and log houses, trees, green grass and a general mountain coolness and freedom, formed a grateful contrast to the tiresome adobe villages and low fields which lay in the valley a few miles away. Nor was the cabin entirely alone. A quarter of a mile away was the large quadrangle of green grass, in the centre of which arose a slender flag-staff, surrounded by houses little better than Joe's, but in which dwelt men and women so far removed from him that he saw them only from afar. Then there were glimpses of white canvas, horses neighed from the long rough sheds, and, as if to guard the bare standard of authority, a sentinel paced back and forth before the flag-staff, and two brass guns stood open-mouthed and glittering on either side. In a word, it was the universal concomitant of settlement and safety throughout the land, a military post. A spot than which it would be hard to find one more green and beautiful, was enlivened all the year by the parade of arms, and the incense of military devotion arose each morning and evening in the sullen growl and lingering blue smoke of a gun at whose sound the deer started and listened, and the rabbit bounded away to his cover in the copse.

But if you followed the road which straggled in indistinctness past Joe's cabin, you would find yourself soon among glades scented with balsamic odors, among rocks which had been rolled from their original beds and tumbled down the hill, and steep hillsides whose red earth showed signs of curious work. It was a land of wild scenes and wilder men, protected only by force from the Apache, where the dwellers even in their worst estate could dream of nothing better. But it was also the land of gold. Where ran the stream in the valley a mile below, the mule drew in an endless circle the rude shaft of the primitive *arastra*. The Mexican patiently worked his cradle with dirt carried thither upon a donkey's back, and over all brooded the restless spirit of American enterprise, wandering, prospecting, speculating and gambling; rough, vindictive, generous, and ever athirst for wild adventure and wealth.

Joe Biggs was that kind of man who needs no particular description to those acquainted with his species in a mining country. He was a Tennessean, so long absent from the land of his nativity that he himself had nearly forgotten the fact. Though still a robust, middle-aged man, he had been for many years a mountaineer, and a victim of all the thousand vicissitudes which here, as elsewhere, befall a man whose principal characteristic is recklessness. It would seem a poor place for domestic troubles, and that any kind of prudence might enable a man to leave them out of his calendar of sorrows. But Joe had not that prudence, and in the appearance and temper of his last wife, he was the most unfortunate man in those diggings. Joe was just that kind of man that is always married—married without any regard to place, circumstances, appearance or compatibility. There are many men like Joe. The world would be deluged with domestic dolefulness if the story-tellers only knew who they were.

Years before, when the mountaineer's tall figure was very straight, and his tawny beard knew no thread of gray, in his saunterings in and about the village, he one day came upon a maid of the nut-brown variety, whose eyes were very black and her bare shoulders very shapely, and as she milked goats in the yard, he leaned upon the wall and tried to twist his Tennessecan dialect into something like Spanish. It is useless to tell the rest. The dead-and-gone beauty had long been among the memories and regrets which men and women everywhere are apt to carry in their hearts. We can not tell what thoughts were at work in Joe's heart as he delved in the mountainside, while the daughter she had left him sat near and watched the work, or how sweet the water tasted which she brought him from the spring, or what weighty and important things were discussed as her lively chatter went continuously on through all the work, and Joe's kindly bass came in between. Fathers and daughters are plenty enough, and all the world knows their proverbial intimacy, and how in this perfect equality of June and December, June is generally the wiser and stronger of the two.

But Joe's last matrimonial venture was of a different kind. She was a long and awkward Texan, one of the kind that are constantly wandering westward, and are ever ready to be married upon a day's acquaintance, to almost any one. Joe must have been demented. He afterwards frequently thought of the circumstance with that extenuating possibility as an excuse, for he came, saw, conquered, and led his angular bride away from the cottonwood beneath which the ceremony had been performed, all within three days from his first sight of her "folks'" camp. Then the mountaineer's troubles began, and after about a year, he staggered home from the trader's store three night's out of the week, in manner and form, and meeting with the same reception, as set forth in the beginning of this history.

So, as the woman comforted her wakefulness with muttered words wnich were only a compromise with profanity, and Joe snored in fortunate unconsciousness of the storm, there was still another person in the cabin, who, more than any of the three, was a sufferer in the habitual misery of drunkenness and domestic strife. The daughter was fifteen years old, which, with such as she, means all the softness, tenderness and beauty of youth, together with the perfect maturity of womanhood. That her training had been thus far peculiar and imperfect, was not her fault, nor that of her uncouth tutor. He was rough and coarse, as his kind ever are, but years of roughness and coarseness sometimes fail to blot out in a man's heart the memory of the time when he was innocent. As he went to delve in the hill-side, ever searching for the yellow dust, and ever finding only enough to feed hope, the child went with him, grasping his big finger with her tender childish clasp. As she lay asleep on his ragged coat in the pine-shadows, while the noon heats baked the bare red hills, the long lashes trailing her flushed cheek, and the withering wild flowers in her little pudgy, tired hand, Joe's heart warmed toward her with a feeling which brought back everything which was good in the youth of a wild life. The mountaineer was not utterly bad, nor entirely weak, and as day by day her fingers twined in his beard, and her love crept into his heart, a consciousness of the greatness of his trust grew upon him. And then the little one had the blood of a generation of East Tennessee mountain virtue in her veins. But Joe never thought of that. The rough miners occasionally saw their neighbor engaged in strange occupations, as they passed by. As for instance, leaning upon his pick, the child's bright eyes studying his face, and forgetful in his earnestness that mountains and trees have ears, he told her of the country and the people where he was born; of coon-hunts and log-rollings; of the few months in which he learned all he knew of the hardness of the benches of a primitive school-house, and more than all of his mother. He tried to make the wondering infant understand that he could have a mother. Nay, more, he ventured to try to teach her again, some of the things that his mother had taught him. Perhaps there were other listeners than the passing miners or the wondering child, as in his blundering way he told her of the Maker of all things, and the Christmas of so many hundred years ago. But in the end he always came unconsciously back to the beginning of his story,—his mother. He seemed to fancy that she might be living yet. " When yer daddy finds a pocket we'll go back there little 'un," he said.

Joe's bad ways had begun but lately, and his daughter, still his companion, but no longer a child, began to have the dawn of trouble in her fair face. Now, when the woman's tongue had abated its vigor, and she too seemed at last to have forgotten her husband's sin in slumber, the girl arose and glided through the open door into the brilliant night. The conventionalities of the world had little place in her life, and as she leaned upon the broken fence and looked down the mountain road, her small feet were bare in the dew, and her round arms lay listlessly upon the topmost rail. She was not conscious of herself as she stood thinking, or that the beautiful light which was so unkind to her step-mother's features, made her face a Madonna's, as she looked up into the blue depths, with the tears on her lashes. By and by, in the vague unhappiness which she could hardly define, and for which she knew no remedy, she laid her forehead upon her arms, and did what woman in all times and races is apt to do,—just cried. It was past midnight. She heard dimly the sentinel's challenge, as the nightly pomp of the "grand rounds" came and passed; the faint clink of arms and the small commotion at the guard-house, as the surly crew fell into line to be counted; and lastly the retreating footsteps and settled silence which proclaimed the untimely ceremony done. She had heard these sounds a hundred times, they were not curious, and she straightway forgot them in her girlish tears.

Presently the sound of a quick footstep came nearer and nearer up the road. It was a jaunty figure that came rapidly towards her as she looked. The crimson sash upon his shoulder proclaimed him only "officer of the day," but it was worn like the baldric of an earl. The moonlight played upon button and epaulet, and kissed the sombre plume in his hat, and flashed up and down the bright scabbard he carried upon his arm. But all this was not so much the fault of Lieutenant Thurston as of the moonlight. He was only a soldier; but he was young, and had the dash which is characteristic of every man who follows the flag and the drum for love of arms. As he came he timed his footsteps to the tune he hummed —something that had in its air a suggestion of life and devil-may-caredness which was strangely at variance with the sleepy hour at which he marched.

The blithesome son of Mars had finished his round as required in regulations, and under the influence of wakefulness and stimulated by the balmy air and the night's silvery splendor, had continued his walk up the mountain road. Was that all? Young men's actions sometimes find unconscious excuses in their hearts. He had often been here before—so often that every gaunt cactus and every stone in the rugged road was a familiar thing. As he came blithely, he always returned thoughtfully. About the hardest thinking the lieutenant did was when he returned from Joe's cabin. Then the remembrance of a house three thousand miles away came into his mind with a tinge of bitterness. He thought of the starchy repectability, the gold-spectacled and precise propriety of the middle-aged gentleman whom he designated as "the governor." Then there was a sister or two, and a circle of acquaintances. But the crowning reflection was, what would mother think?" This lady the lieutenant knew very well, and her prominent characteristics had been long since so thoroughly memorized that he thought with a pang of the pain he might inflict by an alliance with anything which lacked the grand essential of "respectable associations." That there was another side to the question was also true. He was far away from anything which touched family respectability. He was literally owned, and all his hours and movements were directed by the great republic whose uniform he wore. His home was his quarters, his profession his sword. Long years would probably pass before he would even see the home or the people which, little as they suspected it, had now almost passed out of his life.

Joe's daughter was not in the habit of waiting for him by the fence. Not by any means. But the young soldier had reached that stage in which he came so far merely to pass and see the homely house in which lived and slept the creature who was oftenest in his mind. He had often seen her and spent an hour in listening to her lisping English, watching the flushes on her cheek, weighing her tact and evident intelligence, and falling still more deeply in love. But it had always been on casual occasions, and by daylight.

As he espied her, he stopped suddenly in his song, and said as usual, "By Jove!"

She, after hesitating a moment between inclination and a natural sense of propriety, stayed where she was, and the flush on her cheek as he came near was strangely at variance with the tear-marks which were also there.

This rash young man could not have felt more intense pleasure in meeting any of the queens of society than he did then. That was argument enough for him, as it would be to most of us under similar circumstances, as he came near and held out his hand. Then he also leaned upon the fence and looked steadily at the oval face, red and brown, glorified in the moonlight and stained with tears.

"You've been crying," said he.

"Si Senor—yes." And then, grateful for a listening ear, she began to tell of the cause of her unhappiness. And in the attempt, the sense of her sorrows overcame her again, and she laid her head down upon her arms and sobbed louder than ever.

There was indeed but little use for her to do aught but cry. The soldier knew, or guessed the story before. But the effect was such as might have been expected under the circumstances. The pretence of comforting, coupled with a secret desire to have the pretty trouble go on, came to the lieutenant on this occasion as naturally as it does to all men.

"Don't cry," he said. "It will all come right in the morning."

Such miserable platitudes are not expected to amount to anything, and they did not in this case.

"The—the woman beats me," she said, and the sobs became almost hysterical.

Then the platitudes were at an end. "Beats *you?* Did you say—do you mean that yon miserable harridan has ever struck *you?*" and his face grew white with indignation.

"Look here," he continued, as she made no reply," why don't you and the old—I mean your father—cut loose from this sort of thing? You and he can live together, can't you? Go somewhere—do something, but," he added, " don't go far."

Then he came a little nearer—so near that a tress of the girl's loose and luxuriant hair lay beneath his hand. " You must not imagine that because your miserable father gets drunk and the other creature strikes you, that you have no friends. If this kind of thing occurs again we'll make it *warm* for 'em," and then the lieutenant placed his hand caressingly upon a white shoulder.

Perhaps he meant well—we will suppose he could hardly help it, but it was a mistake. The girl arose from her reclining posture, and turning toward him a haughty and indignant face, and eyes that glowed with sudden fire, without a word went into the house.

As Lieutenant Thurston walked slowly homeward, he did not think so much of his mother's aristocratic notions. His mind was intensely occupied with a new idea of the woman he had just seen. Our military friend was just now learning that womanliness, and the virtue that clothes it, regardless of associations or education, is an instinct and an inheritance. Old Joe's beautiful child was not a mere Spanish girl. On this night at least, if never again, her free Saxon blood and her father's homely teachings have served her well. The soldier pondered those things. He was deeply stung, and his face burned with mortification. But he was not an ignoble creature, and his unspoiled manhood and his soldier's honor came to his aid. "If *that* is the kind of woman it is," he mused, "by Jove I can't see what family respectability has to do with it." And he was more deeply in love than ever.

In the morning Joe's spouse awoke sullen and sour, and berated him more than ever. The girl went about with a sad face, over which came at intervals a red flush, which betrayed her remembrance of last night. The miner went away, and the girl stood in the morning sunshine again by the broken fence, and watched the guard-mount afar off, and thought she discerned a tall figure there, and almost wished he would come again. How small her world was, and how large a figure one man could make in it, she never reflected. It is ever so. A woman's world may be filled with the tiniest dot, so she but loves it.

When Joe Biggs came again at noon, he talked to his daughter. "We can't stand this much longer, kin we, Sis?" As she only answered by a look, he continued:

"I've done made up my mind. We'll quit. It wus a mistake o' mine," pointing over his shoulder toward the house with his thumb; "but I meant it well. Do ye mind the place over the mountain I showed ye once when we thus thar? Well, there's a *pocket* thar. How do I know? Well, I don't jest *know*, but this kind o' thing can't last allus—luck 'll come to a man sometime; and I'm a mind to go an' try fur it thar. Git ready Sis; we'll go fur it now—to-night; and mind, now, don't tell *nobody*."

When Lieutenant Thurston passed the miner's cabin, shortly after sunset, he thought he saw a laden donkey whose rider was a woman, far up among the pine shadows on the mountain road. It was indistinct in the gloaming, but the man who plodded behind reminded him of Joe. The matter passed from his mind, and he forgot it in thinking of something he did not see, for the only living thing at the cabin was the woman who sat upon the step, her chin in her bony hands, eyeing him as he sauntered past with the vindictiveness of all her kind towards anything which looks like respectable humanity.

The days passed, and the weeks, and nobody seemed able to answer the question, "where is Joe?" The woman came to the commandant for bread, and declared herself cruelly deserted, and very badly wounded as to her feelings; and finally she departed unregretted with a party of her countrymen, for a land where men were more faithful. As for Lieutenant Thurston, he kept his thoughts, whatever they were, to himself. He was suspected of a careless weakness for "Joe's daughter," and rallied upon that point by his companions. But he seemed to fail to perceive any pleasantry in their careless remarks about the absent girl, and they desisted. It would not be strange if he thought his advice to her that night was connected somehow with her and her father's unexplained departure, and that the character of his last interview with her was such as to render him rather odious to her recollection than otherwise.

The summer months, with their glory of air and sunshine and balm, passed away, and when the earliest snowflakes of mountain winter were sifted over the land, Joe and his daughter seemed wellnigh forgotten. But the dames and gentlemen of the garrison would have been much surprised had they known that the gayest and brightest man of them all—the life of their limited and exclusive gatherings—had a greater regard for the mere recollection of the old miner and his beautiful child than he had for all of them, or any of the names or faces in-the far-away land where he had spent his boyhood and which he still called " home." The lieutenant, his fellow-officers thought, was growing " odd." He borrowed the topographical charts from the adjutant's office and studied the geography of the wild mountain ranges. He questioned the wandering hunters and miners, with the hope that they might tell him something of the persons he was thinking of. But all were ignorant. Joe and his daughter had strangely dropped out of the world.

The young soldier began to think that he had reached that problematical part of life in which a man seems no longer to have any use for himself. He had grown tired of his daily life and his routine of duties. His pleasures had become very tame and insipid, and the winter's inactivity, though only begun, seemed endless and irksome. His constant thought of the miner's daughter, which was the real secret of all this, he excused under the plea of curiosity. More and more, as he thought of it, it seemed possible that by some rare chance he might find her hidden among the hills of that almost unknown stream whose waters ran toward the Pacific thirty miles to the westward. All that men knew of the valley of the Gila then, were stories told by returning explorers of a stream from whose undisturbed current the trout leapt in the tameness of unhunted nature; of uplands smiling in the greenness of almost perpetual summer, and valleys in which the traveller seemed to have entered upon a new world. The hills were full of precious things, and the game which started from every brake made it a kind of a hunter's paradise. Lieutenant Thurston had heard much of this current geography. For a long time he had heard carelessly, but of late it had seemed to offer a fair excuse for getting rid of himself. When he had asked the commandant to organize a scout to march in these regions, and had been refused, he bethought himself of a hunting tour, and asked for a leave-of-absence and an escort. These he managed to obtain, and after three days of careful preparation, with eight men and laden mules, he wended his way through the slush of melting snow up the mountain, where Joe and his daughter had gone before. The man upon whom depended his safety and his future return, was a Mexican guide, who confirmed all the stories of the Gila country, and who had led explorers there, he said, before Thurston was born.

Were this a journal of a traveller's adventures, the frosty solitudes of mountains where, perhaps, a white man had never trod before, might well furnish a page. Men tell of the Adirondacks, and the strange wildness of regions which every summer are the tramping-ground of tourists; but those experiences in which man becomes a companion of the silence which has been unbroken since time was young, are seldom told. The slant winter sunlight lingered along the aisles of pine, and tinged with melancholy glory, white peaks unseen and unnamed before. They drank of snow-born streams which passed in cold and tasteless purity away to unknown depths and distance. The holly hung its drapery of green and crimson upon the hoary ledges, and the greenbriar and bramble lay in matted impenetrability across the cavern's mouth. Immense boulders sat perilously perched on the edges of abysmal depths, seeming as though the mountain wind, or the grey-eagle's nest, or the finger of a child, might hurl them headlong. The hanging creepers and and the gray moss clung with tenacious fingers to dizzy acres of perpendicular granite. Here and there the cold blue depths of a mountain tarn lay silent between gray peaks that had been mirrored there for ten thousand years, and on its oozy edges were the sharp indentures made by the hoofs of the mountain sheep, the round imprint of the wild-cat's cushioned tread, the dog-track of the fox, and hardening in the crust, the curious marks which seem to have been made by some wandering barefoot child, where the stupid bear's cub had come to lap before his winter's slumber. And all was brooded over by a magnificent silence, which seemed the fitting respite to the volcanic thunders which, when the world was new, had strewn the valley with its fire-scarred rocks and thrust the bold peaks into the smoky air. The gray bird of solitude sat upon the crag and plumed his feathers so near that they could see the yellow ring in his relentless eye, and winged his way to his unknown eyry without a sound of wing or voice, and save him there seemed to be no inhabitant of earth or air. In glens so deep and sheltered that only the sun at mid-day looked into their recesses, the hardy mountain flowers still bloomed and the coarse grass was green and brilliant. The ledges dripped with the ooze of melting snow, and the slender icicles which grew each night fell tinkling into the rocky depths in the morning's sun. Only on the far summits where the foot of man shall never rest, winter held unbroken sway. The gathering snow which propped itself against the pines on the mountain-side, broke loose from its fastenings, and tumbled into the valley a fleecy cataract which flung its spray into their faces, and buried an acre in its rest. And then the muffled echoes died away, and the wanderers turned aside to wonder when the hour would come that should wrap them in cold suffocation and chill their faculties into drowsy death.

Lineal distance is not to be measured by mountain wanderings. After many days of devious journeying, the lieutenant knew that the warm fires of the post were blazing scarce fifty miles away. He knew too that somewhere among the rocks, perhaps not a hundred yards away, were the dim trails, the blazed trees, and the remembered landmarks by which men had come and gone before, and which shortened distances and made intricacies plain. But to be lost in the mountains is to be dazed, bewildered, insane. Men lose the faculty of observation, and wander in an endless round. They sit down to final despair, when only a ledge shuts out the sight of home, and the voices of friends might almost reach their ears. The lieutenant was lost. He knew it, and grimly bit his lips. The guide was lost, and while he pretended a familiarity with each shadowy glen, and claimed old friendship with each grim peak's imperturbable face, the leader knew that too. With a contempt for unwarranted pretences which men do not cease to feel even in despair, he addressed the Mexican no word, and himself quietly took the lead. The party rode in silence. The knowledge of the situation was in every man's face except the master's. He gave his orders with the bluff distinctness of the parade-ground. For himself he did not think he cared. He had in his heart the high courage which, regardless of physical strength, is the result of early training in the family, the school, and the traditions of a courageous race. He was one of that throng of gladiators whose strength the world is beginning to understand, and in whom is illustrated the difference between him who saluted Nero in the arena, and him whose keen blade is given him first by his mother, and sharpened afterward at Harvard or West Point, or mayhap only in the common school. Yet this young soldier was not a remarkable man. He was only one of those who are carving out the destinies of a brilliant century through the difficulties of a daily life. He knew that beyond there was an open country, a river, a plain, or some change which could give vision and hope, and as he rode silently at the head of the party, he fixed his eye upon some distant object which might keep them from wandering in the endless circle of bewildered men, and help them to the end at last, whatever that end might be.

So long as the nightly snow melted in the morning sun, they need not thirst. So long as the startled hare sprang up before them, they need not want for meat, and so the commandant led his party on. At night, in some sheltered spot, the blaze of the cedar-boughs threw its ruddy glare into the night's brooding darkness. The fox drew near to wonder at the illumination, and the green light of the deer's bright eye flashed upon them from beyond the illuminated circle. It was a wilderness where even the Indian seemed never to have come, and in the tameness of astonishment the beasts came near to them in seeming friendship.

Then the soldier would leave his companions in the silence of slumber or thought, and wander away among the rocks and shadows. He did not go to brood and think alone. It seemed to him, as it does always to men in such circumstances, that He whose hand had reared these pinnacles came near and filled with His unseen being the sinless solitudes of the primeval world. In his utter helplessness and despair he looked upward through the mighty shadows to the sailing clouds and calm stars, and prayed. Was he then a Christian? No, but he who asks the question may not know that when men utterly lose faith in any power of their own to save, they may reach upward and almost touch the mighty hand. There are hours when no man is an Atheist.

And one night, as he walked in the gloom, he looked back and saw the silent group painted in striking colors by the brilliant light. A faint glow went before him into the darkness, and he seemed to see the outline of a path. A little further and that was again lost, but he thought he detected the faint odor of new-delved earth. Here and there a huge boulder lay in his way, and as he touched them with his hand, he could feel the slimy dampness of that side which had lately rested in the earth of the hill-side. Something white and soft caught upon his foot, and as he stooped and took it up, it seemed to be—a handkerchief. He held it before his eyes, and spread it out in the darkness to verify, if possible, the tremendous truth that it was indeed a link with the world, and then with a new hope, placed it in his pocket. Then he sat down upon the dry, dead pine fringes, beneath an overhanging rock to think. How had a white handkerchief, the very index, not only of civilization, but of refinement, come to be lost here? There was a name in the corner—the faint lines upon the white could be distinguished. But whose? He longed for light to see that human name. He had almost started up to return to the fire, when a strange sound fell upon his ear, and he stopped to listen. It was as a whirlwind heard from far. "It is the wind in the pines," he said to himself, and still listened as it drew nearer and nearer. Then a crackling sound mingled with the roar, and presently a great bulk in the darkness leaped with a dull thump into the valley before him, and rolled along the ground.

Then another fell with a mighty crash almost at his feet, and he crept still nearer the protecting rock. And while the great roar gathered in sound, and the foaming white sea above him came down like a relentless doom, the pallid face and drawn lips of the one frail man who stood in its path were turned away, and as the pall settled at the mountain's base, its cold folds shut in a figure poor and weak as compared with the mighty force which overwhelmed it, but grander, indeed, than all in the capacity for a heroic struggle with death.

In the morning, the soldiers and the guide looked upon a great heap of snow, whose outer edge reached nearly to their camp-fire. "He is dead," said they, as they communed among themselves. At noon, they loaded their beasts again, and started backward towards home. Was it indeed backward? The eagles which watched their wanderings, and the gray wolves which gnawed and scattered their bones, will never tell.

But he was not dead. The shelving rock was upon one side, and the white wall of snow upon the other, and between lay his bed of dry pine leaves. As the hours passed, a blue light came through upon him, and showed him the crystal outline of his hopeless house. He called, and the dull sound he heard mocked his own voice. But he did not lack air; neither was he wanting in energy or hope. He could touch the gray rock and the earth, and they seemed of the world, and friendly. He was hungry, and the blue-white light smote upon his eyes and numbed his brain. As he reflected, he would have given all his knowledge of geography in general— nay, all he knew besides — for the topography of the snowy world in which he was buried, so that he might tell upon which side the white barrier was thinnest.

Then, as the gnawing and weakness of hunger came upon him, he began to delve. He knew that strength would fail in experiments, and where he begun he must continue. As his fingers grew numb and stiff in his work, he wished he might barter all his hopes in life for a despised spade. But his prison was not cold. The snow was a thousand blankets, and the radiating heat of the earth became a steam. As he worked he took the handkerchief he had almost forgotten, to wipe his brow, and as it met his eye, lo! in the corner stood the familiar name, "R. Thurston, U. S. A." Fate seemed now doubly in league with mystery, and as the poor man held the cloth in his cold fingers, his haggard eyes looked amazement.

After hours, the opaline mass grew slowly dark again, and he crawled backward through his narrow tunnel, to warm his hands and rest. Rest came with sleep. "He giveth his beloved sleep," and the angels must have looked kindly upon the spot where, beneath his tapestry of snow, one lonely pilgrim lay like a play-wearied child, with his head upon his arm in tired slumber.

When he awoke he knew from his watch that he had slept five hours. He was frightened to think how the time was slipping away and he had not saved. Hunger waits not upon effort, and already the enemy was insidiously gnawing at his vitals. But he did not immediately set to work again. On the contrary, he did something, which to the uninitiated, would seem the very opposite. He was not utterly without a solace and comforter, and this comforter is one which has accompanied men in much toil and weariness in this world. It comes to every camp-fire, and stills like a balm the cry of hunger and cold. It was a brown pipe. He leaned against the rock, and the incense of the Virginia weed ascended and was absorbed in the roof of virgin snow. After a while a calmer light came into his eyes, and he arose and crept into the narrow tunnel. Lying prone, he gathered the soft snow from above and pressed it beneath him. Wearily the hours passed. Sixty feet—seventy—ninety —a hundred. He looked backward through the long, white passage, and thought of the unknown distance yet to go, and his strong heart almost failed him. A hundred and ten—twenty. His head was dizzy, and the blood from his numbed fingers stained the snow. But he found something which was not white and cold, and drew it forth. It was a dead bird. Even as he lay, he tore it limb from limb and ate its very heart, and then in thankfulness and courage delved again. Ten feet more, and his fingers were as sensitive sticks, and refused their office. Then he crept slowly backward again, and crawling to his couch, tried to chafe his stiffened limbs into new life. Darkness had come again, and he again slept. He did not wake until morning, and then his raw hands were swollen until in regarding them he almost smiled. He crept again into the long tunnel, and with pain at every stroke, worked at his task for life. A huge boulder intervened, and with infinite pains he delved around it. The slow hours passed and he was still another hundred feet nearer the far-off world. He ate the snow from thirst, and the thirst grew as he ate, and now his throat was sore and swollen, until the act of deglutition was a torture. He was chilled, and drowsiness nearly overpowered him. He was afraid to sleep, for he knew that sleep was death. He was weary with a langour which he could not understand, and the narrow backward track seemed too long to be traversed again. Weariness had overcome hunger, and all feelings had given place to utter exhaustion. And still with weary strokes he plied his task. He knew that light must soon come—or death. He could not afford to waste strength in crawling backward to his bed. He could not wind his watch with those swollen and senseless fingers, and the long hours of the night passed uncounted, and still with that mechanical, dogged energy with which strong men fight death, he delved on. Three hundred feet, and when morning again shone dimly through the snow, he hardly noticed, and did not care, that through the mass before him it came stronger and clearer than before. A few more strokes, and then a rest. Then a reviving energy, a little further progress through the icy barrier, and again silence. An hour longer, and the efforts are such as drowning men make when they clutch at ropes which are flung to them too late. There is no perceptible progress now, and the poor wretch cannot even see that through the thin crust the light comes full and strong. A few more convulsive, useless efforts, and the weary head falls upon the outstretched arm, and the last gallant stroke for life fails in the drowsiness which merges soon into an eternal sleep.

* * * * * * *

The January sunshine lights up the little valley with a blithesome glitter, which seems strongly at variance with the snow upon the higher peaks. The air is full of the balm and sweetness which is the characteristic of the southern mountain ranges, and on every hand are the evidences of that strange mingling of perennial spring and eternal cold which in more level countries seems a fable.

Strewn along the edges of a noisy stream are four or

five log houses. The spots of brown earth dot the hillside, the uprooted boulders lie in the valley, and on every hand are the evidences of the miner's work. The settlement, in the very heart of the Sierras, is probably very new, and as yet unheard-of in the world of stocks and trade. Everything necessary to a rude life is carried thither on donkeys' backs, and costs almost its weight in the precious dust, of which there is no small quantity hidden in these cabins. All around lie the peaks and valleys of an unknown wilderness, through which even the miner has not yet wandered. You might pass and repass within a few hundred yards of Biggs's gulch and never suspect its existence. The old man himself and his daughter passed around the spur and near the new snow-bank, about nine o'clock in the morning, on the twentieth of January. It was Sunday; and he carried nothing but a stick. Their errand was not gold this time, but wild flowers for her and trout for him. But, after all, there was something in their errand unsuspected by them. As they passed by, the old man stopped to regard the huge drift which had come so suddenly, and whose outer crust was fast melting away under the rays of the valley sun. As they stood there, his eyes, ever accustomed to notice the small things of nature, discovered a curious cavity in the snow, fast widening in the sun. He stooped to obtain a horizontal view. "Suthin inside begun that hole, Sis, an' the meltin' is a-finishin' of it," he said, and advanced and inserted his stick. At the very entrance it touched something soft. Then he broke away the crust, and there, before their astonished eyes, lay a blue-clad figure, the face downward and resting upon an outstretched arm. It were useless to note the ejaculations of astonishment, some of which had a touch of irreverence, as he drew forth into the sunlight the limp figure, and the bright rays kissed the pallid, suffering face of the soldier who had fought death and was almost conquered. It would have been entirely in order if the girl had screamed and swooned away. She did neither, but her face took at once a rosy flush and a deathly pallor. "Wait a minnit," shouted the old man, somewhat flurried, and started off as fast as his elderly limbs could carry him. As he passed around the spur, the girl still stood looking at the prostrate, unconscious form, and her face showed a curious mingling of emotions. Then her eye caught one bleeding, swollen hand, and as she knelt and lifted it, she began to cry. Then she took the other, and it would seem that she thought to warm and heal them by contact with her fresh, wet cheek. As the moments passed, she drew nearer and nearer to him. She touched his cheek with her's, and pushed back the damp hair. Then she suddenly left him and ran to the bank around which her father had gone, and looked up into the village. No one was coming. She glanced quickly around, and not even a bird was near. Then, as if fearful of the loss of time, she darted back to where he lay, and, kneeling, lifted his shoulders in her arms, and pressed his head to her heart as a mother presses her child. Even as the tears fell upon his face, a rosiness of pity and love overspread her own. She exulted in it. She kissed his closed eyes. "*Ay di mi!*" she said; "poor ting, poor ting!" But even as she caressed and lamented, the soldier opened his eyes. She just laid him down again, and sat apart in utter shame, daring neither to look at him or leave him. Then the old man came with his companions, and as they carried him to the cabin the girl followed far behind.

It is strange, indeed, how near the brink a man may go, and yet return. Another hour in the snow-bank and the soldier would never have seen the sunlight again. As it was, it seemed that the sluggish blood was slow to resume its chilled functions. But as he lay beside the one window of Joe's cabin and looked out upon the varied scene, it seemed that he did not much care. The distant post, guard-mount and dress parade, the midnight tour on the guard-line, his loved profession, and the charm and glitter of arms, all seemed to be far-away and almost-forgotten things. As he lay there, and the strength came slowly back, he was indifferent as to whether his friends knew of his fate or not. He was enjoying the only absolute and unquestioned dominion a man ever has in this democratic world—the dominion of the convalescent. He had almost forgotten his lady mother lately, and the grim terrors of an infringement of the Draconian statutes regarding respectable connections no longer troubled him. Old Joe went his daily way to his shaft, and the demure girl, who sat at the fire and occupied herself with the endless stitching of her sex, was his physician in more senses than one. Sometimes, as he watched her, there was the old merry twinkle in his eye, and a sly smile dawned in his face. Perhaps he was thinking of the handkerchief she had in a manner stolen from him, and the other less useful, but far better things, she had lately given him in return.

But he talked to her, and was rewarded by the interest with which she listened to the strange facts he related. And then he feigned the sulks, and grew tyrannical, and declared that unless she came near, nay, even sat upon the bedside, he would never speak more. Once, when he had her there, he told her of his far-away home, and of his mother and sisters, and then entered largely into the subject, and described even more clearly than her father ever had the characteristics of the two great races of which she was the descendant.

And in the earliest days of spring he walked about the village, much interested, apparently, in the life of the mines. He went with the girl to his last camp, and looked with curious eyes at the ashes. And they two sat down together at the arching rock, and her face flushed, and her bright eyes sparkled with pitying tears as he told her of the nights in the snow. No wonder that he became to her the grand monarch of all thoughts, and the chief end of life. The world of the mountains became beautiful even to her accustomed eyes since he was there. And as for him—well, he had made up his mind.

One day he followed Joe to his hole in the hill-side. They sat together upon a log at the mouth of the shaft. "My friend," said he, "I must go back to the post; will you lend me that mule?"

"Well, now—psho," said Joe, "ye needn't hurry. Besides, ye can't find the way 'thout I go, an' I haint got time."

"I'll find a guide, Joe. Will you lend me the mule?"

"Y-e-s, of course," says Joe; "but," he added, with a sly twinkle in his eye, "how'll I git the animil ag'in?"

"I will bring it to you."

"An' come back ag'in yerself?"

"Certainly."

The old man looked at the younger keenly and inquiringly. He was peculiar in the respect that all his kind are, and cared no whit for his own or any man's dignity. So, between two who understood each other thoroughly, the conversation went on.

"What would *you* come back here ag'in for?"

"*For your daughter!*"

"Don't ye do it, n'less ye come squar an' fair—I advise ye now. I like ye, young man; I saved yer life, an' I'd do it ag'in. But ef ye 've used what I give ye for any purpus or fancy as is n't squar between my folks an' your'n, it 'ud a been better for ye never to come out'n the snow-pile."

"I tell you I will come again, and that I am an honest man, and a grateful one. What I say I mean, and I will perform it, and that is all I have to say," and he arose to go away.

"Hold on, youngster," cried Joe. "I knowed it, but I wanted to make *sartin*. Bless you, I aint *blind!*"

"Does she know it—have you said anything to *her?*" he continued in a lower voice.

"Well,—yes."

"Come wi' me, I want to show ye suthin' purty," and the miner laid hold of the young man's arm, and started back toward the cabin. When they reached there he lit the greasy implement contrived to do duty as a lamp, and crept under the rude bedstead. "Come on," he cried, from unknown depths, and the soldier crept after him and found himself in a kind of cellar, the earthen roof of which was propped by cedar beams, for the cabin had no floor but earth. "This is whar I lived afore I built the cabin on top," said he. "I 've been poor all my life, an' now the luck has turned at last. This is whar I keep the stuff." Then he threw aside sundry old blankets, gunny-sacks and dried skins, and disclosed some half dozen old fruit-cans, three or four large glass jars, such as are used in packing relishes, and some small sacks made of skin. He took up a quart jerkin-bottle, and as he held it to the smoky light, the dull yellow gleam of the crude gold showed it to be full. Then he opened a can, which held the same yellow hoard. They were all full. There, before his eyes, the soldier saw many thousands of dollars. Then the old man sat down upon a broken box, and eyed his treasure, and talked. He told how he had run away from whiskey and a cross woman, and coming to this spot, thought he detected "signs." He made a dug-out, and killed game for food, and opened a drift into the hill-side. He struck a "lead," a rich one—and then unexpectedly came upon a "pocket." He was stricken with fear, as men generally are under such circumstances, and for a month did not even tell his daughter. Day after day he took out the veined and crumbling quartz, sometimes almost pure gold. He crushed it in a hand-mortar, and subjected it to the rude chemistry of the mountains, with instruments of his own contriving, and at night. Then he needed help, and took his daughter into the secret. Finally he induced some wandering miners to settle in his neighborhood for the sake of company and protection. They had all been successful to some extent, but none of them knew his secret. Then he made the startling announcement that he had once been back to the post, and that it was only sixty miles away by his trail. When asked with astonishment what he had gone for, he simply said "quicksilver," and told how his daughter had stayed "cached" in the mountains during the five days of his absence. As he told this astonishing story with the evidences of its truth before him, the soldier wondered if this was not Aladdin, or if he dreamed. "Now youngster," said he in conclusion, "I've told ye this, so that the arrangement need n't be one-sided. I tell it to ye because ye're honest. The pocket is petered, an' it ain't much, but my lead is worth more thousands than I'm willin' jist now to lay myself out on. I'm gettin' old, an' am a goin' to quit." They climbed the ladder and again emerged into the air. As they stood in the sunlight, it seemed more than ever a dream.

But to the old miner must necessarily come some relief after earnest discourse. He turned away at the door, and as he departed, looked back and said: "Ye kin hev the jackass an' be d—d to ye. I only said it to try ye."

The night passed to the lieutenant a wakeful dream. He had unconsciously lighted upon a wonder, and through the moon-lit hours he tossed, questioning if morning would find all those jars of yellow metal real things. The wealth of this poor girl of the mountains exceeded the most extravagant dreams of moneyed respectability, but did it alter the case? Aside from it all, was he content to forego all there was in the world he had left for her? A week ago he had deliberately concluded upon his course, and he was astonished to find himself questioning his heart now.

In the morning the donkey stood at the door, accompanied by a companion. The lieutenant was assured that the miner, who was to accompany him would not lead him astray, and as he started out, the girl stood in the door, shading her eyes with her hand, and pleasure and regret striving for the mastery in her face. She knew he would return. He had found time and means to tell her that, and woman-like, she believed him. In truth she did not see why he should not, under the circumstances. A young woman need not be expected to understand the mysteries of a life she has never known.

They met the old man in the path. He had not much to say, but as they passed on, he shouted after them; "When you come bring me some quicksilver." The whole affair was to him mere matter of fact.

For two days they plodded steadily on, the soldier paying little heed to the road, and absorbed in his own thoughts, following in the trail of his leader. On the morning of the third day he caught sight of the floating banner on the flag-staff, and the sight gave him a choking sensation. When he alighted at his quarters they were occupied by another, and the whole garrison from the commandant down, gathered round him, and looked at him as one risen from the dead. He briefly told them his story, saying nothing of the personality of his rescuers. He learned then that his companions had not returned. But he had grown accustomed to startling things, and was not surprised. He had been dropped from the rolls, and his military record closed, as one dead. Even that failed to shock him. That night the commandant received a communication, addressed through him to the Secretary of War, tendering Lieutenant Thurston's unconditional resignation, and at the end was the startling declaration, that after so long an absence he had returned to the post only to perform the act necessary to a soldier's honor.

That night he locked his door and read his letters. There was one from his mother, and two or three from female friends. He read the delicate lines, and the faint perfume of home touched his senses. But he laid them on the fire, and moodily watched them turn to ashes. Probably they were never answered.

Four slow weeks went by, and the communication came which ended forever his military career. He carried it to his quarters and locked himself in, and tried to realize his situation. He had been lost in the mountains; he had looked frozen death in the face in the snow-drift. In a few weeks he had tasted nearly all there is in life. But through it all there was no moment so full of regret as this.

Then, at the trader's store there was the busy outfitting of a train of mules with all things necessary in a mountain life, and clad in homely gray, with slouched hat and spurred heel, citizen Thurston directed the enterprise. To the last he told no tales, and as the tinkling procession passed the ruined cabin which had always been known as "Joe's house," the blue-clad throng looked their last upon a man who had once been one of them, and who at that moment passed out of their world forever.

There is a certain town on the far Pacific coast which has grown up in late years with the strange strength which is born of traffic in a hitherto almost unknown country. There is an elegant mansion there, and its proprietor is reputed to be immensely rich. Within are luxurious carpets, and shining wood, and plate glass. The oranges ripen in the yard, and rare flowers bloom on the terrace. He is a scholar, too, and a man not alone of luxurious tastes, but of extensive attainments. But he is mostly envied because he has a beautiful wife. The curious people who have scrutinized her elegant apparel have also noticed that she speaks English with a little lisp, and apparently regards her husband in the light of a demi-god. But they little know how the lady has changed under the tireless lessons of love, and how the mountain nymph became at last the cultivated woman.

And the man who sometimes thoughtfully looks at the old sword and crimson sash, which hang somewhat out of place over the mantel-piece, himself scarcely realizes how much he has accomplished, and how far in the past and valueless, is the respectability which comes by birth and education, compared with that which by faithfulness end honor, and sometimes through danger and suffering, a man may make for himself.

WOMAN UNDER DIFFICULTIES.

THAT embodiment of beauty, gracefulness and kindness, who is at once our ideal and our possession, fills daily our sole conception, our full measure of belief, as to what a woman ought to be, and is. Surrounded by all the appliances, traditions and results of many hundred years of civilization, it is hard for us to conceive of any creature worthy of the blessing of love or the dignity of motherhood, other than our own mothers, wives and sisters.

But no creature is so entirely susceptible to surrounding influences, to the strong teachings of nature, wildness and loneliness, to rough associations and uncouth companions, yet still preserving the great distinctive characteristics which belong to sex rather than to race, as is woman. The women we know and daily see, whom it is a part of our religion to respect, and a part of our life to love, are only typical women—specimens of the grade of beauty and refinement attainable under the highest form of civilization. There are thousands of others, worthy and womanly in their way, who are not as these. Nay, our ideals are scarcely even in the majority.

There are many rough and honest men, whose faces are brown and bearded, and whose hands are hard with toil, who have never even seen the creatures whose white shoulders gleam through *tulle*, whose footsteps patter on errands of extravagance over every paved street, and whose fair faces bloom in rows at the theatre. There are many men in whose early recollections are not included the ineffably genteel "swish" of the matronly silk, as it passed up the church-aisle of a Sunday morning, in the decorous company of fair broadcloth and a gold-headed cane. To him, the being who blushes at the mere insinuation of an indelicacy, whose hair is indeed a "glory," whose palms are pink, whose garments are a triumph, whose movements are tempered with gracefulness, and whose very words are the result of culture, is one so far from his life that he would scarcely picture her in his imaginings of angels.

But he has his companion, like him, and eminently suited to him. In his home, and his wanderings throughout the frontier, he needs no other. Neighbor she has none. Crowded street, the jam and jostle of the pavement, she knows nothing of. Her amusements are lonely, her occupations masculine and homely. All she has, and most that she hopes for, are included in the dull routine of one room, one hearth, one changeless scene. Life to her is the rising and the setting sun, the changing seasons, the cloud, the wind, and the falling rain. She knows the tricks of horses, the straying of the herd, and all the economy of the corral. Business to her is the small traffic of the trading-post. Strangers are those who occupy the white-tilted wagons which she sees come and go on the far horizon. Friends are all who have white faces and Christian names, and enemies those whose faces she seldom sees, and who are the wily and inveterate foes of all her race. Of such as these, the denizens of cities know but little, and they deserve a history from their very isolation.

Wherever the frontiersman has occupied a place in Western annals, his wife has stood in the background. The women of the Plains, of Colorado, of Arkansas and of Texas are of the same genus with the pioneer women of the Wabash and Missouri, only of a more modern stamp. All of them differ in character from the "piney-woods" maiden, whose life, appearance and general character became much better known to us through the veracious narratives of Sherman's "bummers." But men who write of buffalo-land, who wind off narratives of Western life for trans-continental newspapers and magazines, or who verbally detail to a knot of listeners their Othello-like adventures, have little to say of the daughters of the wilderness. The sun-burned and slip-shod woman who hunts cows in the creek "bottoms" upon a bare-backed mustang, who folds her brown hands behind her at the cabin-door, and in a shrill voice gossips with the passing stranger, and whose careless cookery furnishes forth a bill-of-fare as changeless as time, does not figure largely in the romance and the adventure of the frontier.

Why should she? Her precise pattern in these respects still lingers amid encroaching fields, in the ague-haunted fens of the Wabash, and in the sand of the Missouri bottoms. But there are other and more remarkable characteristics pertaining to the woman of the Far West. She is there not from indolence, but necessity. Her surroundings are not a choice, but a misfortune. Indolence and innate untidiness are not the causes of her poor larder and her comfortless home. There is no broad line drawn between her and thrifty and prosperous neighbors. For hundreds of miles, there are no better homes than hers, and with a patience which might have a touch of sublimity were it not so nearly unconscious, she waits for better things. And when those better things come, if they ever should; when population and prosperity encroach too near, then, following the instinct of migration, for God's purposes are as strong in humanity as in the beasts, she and her husband would move again. The grotesque procession of lean and weary cows, multitudinous and currish dogs, rough men, barefoot girls, and lastly the dilapidated wagon, with its household goods, wends never eastward.

The sod-house of far Western Kansas, the cabin of Texas, and the adobe of Colorado, are not all so fortunate as to have a female occupant. The fact is proclaimed by an essential difference in appearance afar off. There never was yet a lonesome borderer who planted a vine, or draped a window, or swept the narrow path in front of his door. The virtues of good housewifery are, in a greater or less degree, the natural qualifications of every woman. In many a wilderness nook, the blooming plant which is cherished beside the door, the drapery of the one small window, the clean-swept hearth, the row of shining tins, and the small evidences of needle-and-thread proclaim that however poor the place may be, if it hold a woman, her hand will still find something to do in the way of adornment.

There is nothing strange in the fact that the Indian squaw is always a slave. But the savage goes but little farther in that direction than his enemy, the frontiersman. In all times, races and circumstances, in which crudity and toil preponderate over ease and refinement, woman bears the burden of the misfortune. But the rule of compensation exists everywhere. The sun and the wind are kinder than are late hours and furnace-heated chambers. The slavery of the field is infinitely more conducive to strength and happiness than the slavery of the corset and high-heeled shoe. Maternity is not a terror and a peril to the woman of the border.

Life, with all its hardship and isolation, gives to her at least all it has to give. The days may be days of toil, but the noon brings its hunger and health, and the night its deep sleep of rest and peace. That wearying round of ceremony, that daily attendance upon the mirror and weekly investigation of the fashion-plates, that thought of Mrs. Smith's bonnet, and Mrs. Brown's children, and the bank-account and the milliner's prices,—all the unseen and untalked-of, yet wearisome and monotonous burdens of fashionable, even civilized life, are here unknown. And the compensation is great. Untrammelled by stays and ceremonies, the border-woman has what few of her race but she entirely possess, health. Not a fictitious and deceptive rosiness of cheek and gracefulness of carriage, not whiteness of hands and willowy slenderness of waist, but coarse, awkward, brawny health. The women who, all over the Eastern United States, are the chief adornment of beautiful homes, and are the wives and daughters of Christian gentlemen, who cause mankind to forget Eden and Eve, and scarcely to remember the fall, and who are the mothers of daughters who are as brilliant as June roses, and who fade like them, and sons who are men at twenty and very old at forty, are not expected to credit all this, or to have the slightest desire for an exchange of circumstances, which to them would be impossible. The facts are only mentioned to show that the pity for those who live thus is often misplaced, and that there is no circumstantial misfortune which has not also its reward.

I know of no female inhabiting the border wilderness of our country who has not some of the refinement which belongs rather to sex than to race, except the Indian squaw. A woman whose face bears any evidence of a relationship with any of the dominant races of the world, has something about her wherever you find her which is womanly and attractive. The borderer's wife does not swear, nor chew tobacco, nor offer any suggestion of immodesty in action or word. The face is not more coarse or more incapable of that surging rosiness which explains the subtle connection between the sensibilities and the circulation, than is the tattling index to a woman's heart the world over. But if I might be allowed to coin the expression, I would say that the standard of delicacy by which the border-woman's sensibilities were governed was a different and broader one than that in common use. She associates with men, and very coarse ones. She is intimately acquainted with and interested in all their affairs. She is accustomed to wildness and danger, and learns to be strong of hand and nerve, and to be cool in sudden emergencies. It may be put down to her credit that while she will run if she can, she will fight if she must. But there are no circumstances which, even by long habit, can divest a woman of her essential feminineness. I have been amused to note that a woman who was complete mistress of a recalcitrant mustang, and every day brought him under subjection by a no means dainty application of the end of his lariat, and who ruled with a high hand all the denizens of the corral, would utter the little cry of her sex and ingloriously retreat at the sight of one of the harmless lizards which infest the prairie-paths of the south-west.

In society, women dress for women; in certain other walks in life, they dress for men; and left alone, they dress for themselves. The story of the first garment ever made out of the new world's fresh green leaves tells only a part of the story. Here on the border, the old business of the sex, to look pretty, receives as much attention as it does anywhere. There is not much choice of material, —calico is the article. Valenciennes and Mechlin, and all the cunning variations in name and material which make up the lexicon of the modern dry-goods clerk, even the cant about "chaste" colors and "pretty" styles, are utterly unknown to the belle of the border. As she tilts back in a hide-bottomed chair like a man, it is easy to perceive that feet which are not always coarse are encased in brogans, constructed with a special view to the roughness of wayside stones, the penetrating qualities of early dew, and the gravity and persuasiveness of kicks administered by them. The neck, sunburned, but not always wanting in due proportion and natural whiteness, is ignorant of collar or confinement. Waist and limb are unconfined by any of the devices which are supposed to be so necessary to style, and the hair, combed straight and smooth, is twisted into a tight little knot behind, which, as compared with the enormous mysteries which for these many years have been carried about beneath the hats of fashionable women, remind one of the knob on an old-fashioned bureau drawer. In a frontier toilet, there is a lack of the two essentials of starch and whiteness. Cleanliness there is to be sure, but it is a cleanliness of material and fact, and fails in any suggestion of daintiness. It is upon the calico mentioned that the efforts of taste are mostly expended. There are ruffles there, and bias stripes, and flounces, and a hundred pretty and fantastic devices which it is beyond masculine technology to describe. Yet there are no prescribed fashions for these vagaries in dress. Each woman expends her ingenuity according to her ideas of beauty. The style of a calico gown may seem a small item in describing the characteristics of a class, but the adornment is so universal that it becomes a feature. It is infinitely to her credit too, being the evidence that barbarism is not the result of hopeless seclusion, and that taste and care will hold a place in the hearts and efforts of woman in her struggle with wildness, until that time shall come in which civilization shall complete her task.

If anything said thus far would lead to the impression that comeliness, not to say beauty, is impossible with the women of the border, the impression needs correction. Under the severest tests, the frontier has a comeliness of its own. It is not the paltry prettiness of gait and manner; not the charm of suave words and cultured address. These make us imagine beauty, indeed, where there is none, and procure gentle thoughts and husbands where there is nothing else to recommend. Frontier charms, where they exist at all, make models of stalwart, untrained grace. Health itself is beauty, and that unfashionable kind is common enough. It were well if absolute ugliness everywhere were the result only of hardship and decay, and on the frontier it is pleasant to think that youth seldom wants its round curves and its crimson glow. There are women here whose hair falls in troublesome abundance and will not be confined; whose cheeks, if they could but know the absence of the caresses of the sunbeams and the boisterous kisses of the wind, would show the clearest white and the bonniest bloom. There are limbs which shuffle slip-shod along trails in search of lost animals, of whose round strength the owner has little thought, and arms which split firewood and bring water from the spring whose whiteness and mould would fit them rather for the adornment of golden clasps and folds of ancient lace. To see these women is to know that the old-time talk about "unconscious beauty" is a fallacy. The consciousness of beauty, and due appreciation and use of it, is its great aid in the absolute enslavement of mankind.

For so long have womankind been accused of an inborn love of gossip, that mankind, in their haste to accept ill-natured doctrines, are ever ready to concede the truth of the statement that she can not exist without it. I am satisfied that in some sort of poor way she can manage to get along without a next-door neighbor. It is stranger still, that when by an extraordinary chance the cabins of two neighbors are in sight of each other, the fact seldom adds anything to the mutual happiness of the female occupants. Do they often see each other—do they waste kisses when they meet—are they inseparable friends? There is not a surplus of any of these things. Two women, here as elsewhere, with no third or fourth party to divert attention, are not apt to love each other with fervor. What is better, they do not pretend to. But neighborship bears a broad meaning in these regions. The chronicle of Brown's wife's affairs is reasonably well kept by Thompson's wife, who lives from twenty to fifty miles away. All this without any facilities for what is usually termed gossip. The wayfarer who has lost a pony, or who wanders in search of straying cattle, is the disseminator of the most valuable items of neighborhood news. As he sits on his horse in front of the door, with his knee upon the pommel and his chin in his palm, he relates how he has "heerd" so and so. And in return, the dame delightedly tells of her own affairs, the "old man's" luck, the measles, the "new folks," and always ends with, "tell Mis' Jones to come over." These things, and much more, the simple cow-hunter tells to "Mis' Jones." But that lady does not "come over." That is a mere form gone through with for politeness' sake. Sometimes she may, but not for the visit's sake. Here as elsewhere there are mysterious gatherings in the middle of the night, and the cry of infancy is heard in the morning. If it were not for their babies, these curious "neighbors" would probably never have any other acquaintance than that which comes about by proxy.

The life of the woman of the border takes still another coloring from the fact that while it is transient it is still her choice, and the lot to which she was born. She and her male companion never think of that fact, and are themselves unconscious of the wandering instinct of the class to which they belong. If they were placed in an Eden they would not wait to be thrust out by an angel with a flaming sword. But the spot they leave never again returns to native wildness. While there, they have accomplished a certain purpose as the forerunners and videttes of civilization. Their home is the wilderness, and they come next after the savage as occupants. Slowly they creep up the valley of the Arkansas, already almost too tame for them. The twinkle of their camp-fires, and their rude homes, dot the verge of wildness in Western Texas. Past the Western forts, over a road which stretches like a path through hundreds of miles of barrenness, they straggle towards Arizona and far-off California. Everywhere, in sheltered nooks, are located the rude homes where they have stranded, waiting for a return of the migratory determination. Each one is the centre of those surroundings and appliances which are the absolute necessities of existence. But they make no better homes. They did not come to stay, and as they repeat the old story of "a better country beyond," they little know that, with a different meaning and in another sense, they tell not only their own, but the story of restless, wandering, longing humanity everywhere.

Thus does woman take her part in a most unexpected place in the struggle of existence. It is not an unimportant one. She brings into the world a constant levy of recruits, to be trained in infancy to wandering, if naught else. It is no strange statement to say that without her the final accomplishment of the end for which isolation, wildness and poverty are endured, could not be attained. In that which we call life, she occupies but a poor place. Her character, her notions, and the incidents of her daily life are so far from the absorbing interests which occupy the denizens of the great world of churches, schools, banks, gas-light and society, that they are scarcely the subjects even of curiosity. But she is still a woman, and a specimen of the capacities of her sex in the exercise of that virtue which, more than any other that is characteristic of woman, is unmentioned and unappreciated,—the virtue of silent endurance. If her hard life on the far border lacks idyllic interest, and needs to cover its hard outlines with the purple garment of romance and poetry, it is a compensating reflection that with its unconscious purpose it still goes on, and that with the carelessness and independence of all her kind she reciprocates the indifference of the world.

THE REUNION OF THE GHOSTS.

THE place had certainly nothing attractive about it, for it was only a dingy chamber within adobe walls. But among the wild hills, it indicated humanity, and human feelings and associations. Compared with the abounding dreariness,—the mountain, rock and sage,—it seemed a cosy and pleasant place. So would anything, that but shut out the all-night chatter of the coyote, or afforded a sense of sucurity from the Apache. Behind it, down the slope, straggled the single squalid narrow street of the Mexican village, ragged and shadowy in the moonlight, with here and there a dull glimmer through an open door; now and then a lone straggler bent on love or mischief; and oftenest a family group, snoring in the sweet repose of poverty in front of their dwelling. Far enough away to express a want of sympathy with its associations, stood the quadrangular enclosure whose white walls fairly glittered in the yellow light, and above which rose the slender flag-staff like a line of white against the blue beyond. The two small guns above the arched sally-port, dutifully polished each day, repaid the labor by a metallic and warlike gleam each night. Below them paced back and forth, erect, soldierly, and silent as the ghost of Hamlet's father, the sentinel, whose weapon glittered as he turned, as only bayonets can glitter, and whose measured footfall was the only sound.

Ten o'clock at night in the borders of the tropics. The cool wind of the Sierras came freshly through the open door, and flared and guttered the candles upon the rude pine table. It was a place renowned in border history, the spot around which cluster (save the mark!) the pleasantest recollections of the frontiersman's and the soldier's life,—the sutler's store at a military post. The gregariousness common to humanity everywhere finds opportunity and expression there. It is the club-room of the wilderness. It is half store and half hotel. It is the rendezvous of the mule-driver and the mail-carrier, and from its dingy boxes are distributed the precious letters from home. Hither, too, sometimes comes a little of the month-old news from the world two thousand miles away; the beautiful world in which live the mother, the brother and the sweetheart, from whose midst went the handsome youth with a blue coat and a sabre, to live thereafter the life of a soldier, and to find his happiest hours in such a spot as this.

Wherever there is military protection,—which means also military authority,—republicanism is lost sight of, and monarchy begins. Every army is a despotism, and the rule it lives by it dispenses to others naturally. Here, on everything movable and immovable, is stamped the gigantic monogram, U. S., and he who as a business wears its uniform and executes its orders, is frequently loved, always feared, and generally dispenses a justice so impartial, and a punishment so swift, that it is a credit to the flag he follows and the mighty, though far-away, power he represents. In scenes and surroundings such as this, have been learned some of the lessons which afterwards aided in the command of mighty armies, and made lieutenant-generals and presidents.

But if in duty your solder is faithful, socially he is as gregarious as the Mexican who, for want of better company, is long since asleep with his asses in the adjoining corral. There are five of them here to-night, young and old, as they have been every night for weeks, and according to custom and dignity, they have the apartment to themselves. Casino and California-Jack have lost their charms from sheer monotony, and lounging and chattering have been the order since ten o'clock. The blouse may be donned and "duty" forgotten at "tattoo;" but there are two things in which your regular is never "off,"—to swagger when he is up, and to tell yarns when he is down. The army officer's strut is as much a characteristic as is the Tipperary trot, and "Captain Jinks" is not entirely a myth. These men were all lounging and gossipping. All but one; for, like the Indian at the feast, there is always one man on duty. This unfortunate individual is the "officer of the day," and he, in plumed hat and glittering bullion, wandered about, clanking his sabre against the furniture, and maliciously congratulating himself that Brown must suffer to-morrow.

These men had nearly all a military history, and held their commissions from the fact of having, like the great majority of American soldiers, taken a gallant part in the gigantic fact of war before they had seen the preparatory school. There was a grizzled fellow who had fought on the Peninsula in an Italian uniform, and had in his trunk a Victoria medal. Though more reticent than his younger companions, he had to-night, for two entrancing hours, told of Garibaldi and Victor Emanuel, Kearney and McClellan, and ended with wishing himself in Cuba and anathematizing the "blarsted country," after the fashion of his nation. Then followed another, whose amours were as numerous as his battles, though he had exchanged an eagle for two bars from mere love of arms. He descanted upon Spottsylvania and the Wilderness, and longed for a "mixture" with that unhappy old country twenty miles to the southward, across whose boundary-line he could march his company in a single day. There are personal incidents of a great war which never find their way into books, and as these old soldiers talked they became Othellos, and were invested with that peculiar charm which in all times and places has commanded listeners, which has made Desdemonas of women, and turned the hearts of peaceful men, with a feeling akin to love, to the emblems and associations of heroism and danger and daring.

There were two men there who, while they had not the tales of love and war to tell, yet were unwilling to let the conversation flag. "Youngsters," in the army, accept the designation with complaisance, not having served that immense number of years which are necessary both to experience and the drawing of a longevity ration. While petted in the main, they are also liable to wholesome lessons, some of which at first go hard. Incidentally and innocently one of these turned the conversation upon the tabooed subject of a man's personal feelings midway between the crest of a long hill upon the top of which was a battery, and at the bottom no reserve, and finally ventured a remark as to the elements and characteristics of personal courage.

The old man listened awhile with fast augmenting impatience, and finally rising to his feet and bringing down his fist upon the table he said: "Wait till you get there youngster, and you'll find there is *no such thing as courage.*"

Charles Henry crossed his slender legs, and looked with polite astonishment at his interlocutor. He probably had not expected so much from such a quarter. "You're joking, Major," said he.

"No, I'm not. I've never said so much before; but having an interest in your welfare for your governor's sake, I want to say to you that if you think it's mere courage that wins battles, you are as much mistaken as if you had forgotten to 'soak' your month's pay-account."

The man of Gettysburg, across the table, looked as though he regretfully assented, and Grizzly went on:

"I'm not saying *you'd* run,—few men ever do. But daylight affords no test. You stay there because men are looking at you. Try it in the *d-a-r-k!*" The old soldier uttered the last word in a stage whisper, by way of emphasis, and dropped into a seat, very red in the face.

It required no great brilliancy to perceive that the theme was a haunting one to him, and that he had some special reason for urging the point, though silent upon it ever before. His companion across the table kept a suggestive silence, and leaning forward with extended finger the speaker inquired:

"Is not that so?"

Gettysburg nodded his head, conclusively, several times, remarking, "You're right, old man."

Grizzly gained confidence from the assent of his friend, whom he had known in the same brigade in Virginia, and as he continued to speak, the said assent was evidently his encouragement in laying himself out upon a question which seemed to be one of his established, though hitherto silent, beliefs.

"I've a mind to tell you something," said he again, "which has been on my mind for years. It is far enough gone now, and after the thing is out, if any man here can explain it, or say he wouldn't have done the same, I'm ready to resign. There are things which happen to a man once or twice in his life which don't belong to the common order. I could scarcely imagine myself caring much about them if they could be seen, but they come in the *night*. What can a man depend upon when he can't see? He can feel, that's true;" and the speaker held out his right hand and looked at the palm thereof with a critical expression.

"I've worn some uniform or other for a great many years," he continued, "and since I joined this miserable little army of *yours*, I've had less to complain of in the way of fighting, and more downright, horse-killing rest, than I've ever been used to. You think I can't stand it long? I can, though; I *rather* like it. I'm certain I don't want any more Wildernesses in *mine*,—a place, by the way, you needn't talk so much about, [to his comrade across the table,] seeing several thousand, including me, were there along with you.

"Speaking of the Wilderness, I never think of it but it reminds me of the peculiar—*very* peculiar—circumstance which I started to tell. From that circumstance, I'm convinced of the truth of what I said awhile ago, when you all thought me preaching; that we are all,—demme, I should think I ought to know,—all *cowards in the dark!* Heard the same remark before, have you youngster? Yes. Well, wait till *you've* tried daylight, before you begin to quote maxims to *me*. I didn't pretend the remark was original."

Thus snubbed, C. A. soothed his feelings with a cigarette, and relapsed into silence.

"You remember the pines in that country,—thick as they can stand and big as your body,—and the old tobacco hills still visible, that were made there before they sprouted, I suppose. Well, one evening it was my turn to post the pickets along the outer edge of one of those interminable pineries which lay between head-quarters and the front. As I rode along in the dusk I could occasionally see the other line, in some places not two hundred yards away, across the clearing. It rained; one of your misty, soaking Virginia rains, such as put out fires, and dampen blankets, and soak a man until he has no relish for water,—'specially as a beverage,—for a week. Before I could get to the end of the line it began to grow dark, and very soon you couldn't see your horse's ears. The rain came down as fine as spray, and when I'd got fairly among the trees, Egypt itself couldn't have been blacker. The fine tassels struck me in the face as though they meant it; and I jammed my knees and scraped my elbows, and wandered and boggled, until finally I began to know for a certainty that I was adrift and very nearly afloat. You've heard pines whisper. Everybody has, I suppose; but that is in daylight, and don't express anything like that night. Why, man, they fairly talked. When I stopped to feel about me and consider matters, you know, I could hear them say: 'O, look at him! look at him! fie, fie, fie!' all in a whisper. You may all think this is foolishness,—and it is now; but it wasn't then. Sometimes I thought I could hear people talking, and sometimes something would crack, as though a twig were trod upon. That's the point to this business. Put yourself in the dark with something that moves and makes noises, and yet that you can't see and can't account for, and any of you will get out of there if you can. Well, I began to think I might chance to get across the line, and the Johnnies would take me in out of the rain and provide for me; and as sure as I live, I had rather have had it happen than stay where I was. I was getting creepy, for it seemed to me I was bewitched. The words the pines whispered seemed plainer than ever, and my hair almost rose on my head when my horse snorted and shied, and stopped dead-still. I struck him with the spurs, but he would n't stir an inch; and moved to desperation, I dismounted, and leading him slowly along, held my hand as far as I could reach before me, and attempted to *feel* myself out of the scrape if I could. He came along well enough then, and I proceeded a rod or two among the trees. Suddenly,— it makes me shiver to think of it,—I placed my bare hand fair against—— what do you think? No, it *wasn't* a tree. Demme, I struck it with my open palm as fairly as though I'd tried to,—a clammy, bearded face! Bah! It was wet and cold and soft, and a finger went right into one staring open eye! Gentlemen, I could feel my hair rise and my heart stop for an instant. What was the thing? Go find one and touch it, and see if you can tell. I know it was a *face*,—a human face,—and that it was cold and bearded and confoundedly unexpected. I backed out of that rapidly for a rod or two, and listened and heard nothing. Then I crouched down behind a tree and held my horse by the rein, and waited through the mortal hours of the longest night I ever knew. The pines kept up their frightful whispering, and except that, there was not the slightest sound. When at last morning came, I found I was three miles from my own camp, and opposite that of another brigade. O, I was brave enough *then*, and so disgusted that to this blessed night I 've never mentioned the circumstance."

"Well, ah—what was it?" ventured Charles Augustus.

"Nothing! Demme, it was a *ghost!*" roared old Grizzly. "I looked everywhere in the morning, and there was absolutely nothing there, living or dead,"

"Yes there was," said a voice from beyond the table "and to this time I have been wondering who or what *it* was, that placed a clammy, wet hand squarely upon my face and then vanished, that night when I stood against a pine in the rain, with my company somewhere on picket,—I didn't know where,—I listening and watching for something that was creeping nearer and nearer until finally I was touched as I tell you."

"But,—but demme! what became of you?" roared Grizzly, rising up, "and why didn't you speak of this before?"

"I had immediate business in the opposite direction," remarked the ghost, dryly.

"You don't mean to say you,—demme you certainly didn't r—"

"Yes, I ran the *other* way, and at this distance I'm not sure I wouldn't do it again. There's no use talking, old man; we won't run *tonight*, and it'll take an hour or two to recover the comfort we sacrificed there on each other's account."

When the moon sets, Charles Augustus in under the table, and Grizzly snores in a corner. Brown, who is officer of the day in the morning, reposes on the counter with his boots on, while the plumed and buttoned individual actually on duty sits in solitary and sorrowful dignity, amid the wreck of matter and the fumes of wine, grumbling at the fates that have decreed that of all throats his alone should be dry, and wondering that the spirits which haunted the Wilderness a decade ago should prove such valiant wine-bibbers four thousand miles from the scene of their wanderings.

COYOTES.

HE has been called an "outcast" by a notorious poet. He is universally conceded to be a sneak, a thief and an arrant coward. He is a worthless vagabond; a wanderer o' nights and a lier-by by day; a dissipated wretch in whose whole history there is not one redeeming fact. He has an extensive connection but no family. He is disowned by the dogs, and not recognized at all by respectable foxes. The gaunt gray wolf who sends his hoarse voice across the ravine, in a howl the most dismal and harrowing that ever disturbed midnight and silence, will have no fellowship with the little thief who seems to have stolen his gray coat, and would fain be counted among his poor relations.

And yet the coyote is the representative animal of the border. It is his triangular and elongated visage; his sharp muzzle, fitted for the easy investigation of the smallest aperture into other peoples' affairs; his oblique, expressionless eyes, which should have a place in the adornment of escutcheons, and the embellishment of title pages. The buffalo, who is his successful rival in such matters, occupies the place because his shaggy, stupid head is big. The buffalo is not the representative of anything but stupidity and ponderosity. He has roamed in countless thousands here, for hundreds of years, and during all that time he has never even bellowed. There is no amount of pleasure, excitement, anger or love, which can induce him to make a sound other than a guttural groaning which ill becomes his size. That great armament of lungs and throat and nostrils is good for nothing in accoustics, and while he might make the valleys to tremble, and his voice might almost shake the hills, he just spends his life in galloping, butting sand-banks and eating. Especially does he affect the latter; his life is one long process of deglutition and rumination. He never stole anything. He never made the moonlit hours hideous, from love of own voice. He is so dull as to be incapable of self-defense. None but a great booby would deliberately run along-side of a slow-going railroad train, to be shot by kid-glove sportsmen, and even by women, three or four score times in the back with silver-mounted pocket-pistols. The stupidity of his whole family is illustrated every day by the countless bleaching skulls, and brown tufts of faded hair, which mark his death at the hands of people to whom the riding of a mustang would be an impossible thing, and the death of a timorous hare, a prodigy of skill and cunning. He has been killed in countless thousands thus, within pistol-shot of a track where with shriek and roar, four trains a day pass, freighted with puny enemies who would never see, much less kill him, if he would only betake himself to the fastnesses of the wilderness which has been his from time immemorial.

Not so his companion and actual master, the coyote. He will lengthen out the days of his life, until his voice sounds hollow and thin and aged, in the watches of the night. Nothing less than infinite pains and insidious strychnine will end his vagabond life. As his gray back moves slowly along at a leisurely trot, above the reeds and coarse grass, and he turns his sly face over his shoulder to regard you, he knows immediately whether or not you have with you a gun. The coyote is a reflective brute, and has an enquiring mind. Only convince him of the fact that you are unarmed, and he procceds to interview you, in a way which for politeness and unobtrusiveness is recommended as a model to more intelligent and scarcely less obtrusive animals.

As he sits himself complacently down upon his tail at the summit of the nearest knoll, and lolls his red tongue, and seems to wink in your direction, he is so much like his cousin the dog, that you can hardly refrain from whistling to him. Make any hostile demonstration, and he moves a few paces further and sits down again. Lie down in the grass, and remain quiet for an hour, and by slyly watching him from the corner of your eye, you will discover that he has been joined by a half dozen of his brethren and friends. Slowly they come nearer and nearer. They are cautiously creeping upon all sides of you. Our curious friend has an object in this, outside of mere foolish curiosity. He is conscious of the frailty of life, and knows that all flesh is grass, and now wants to find out, first, if you are dead, and second, supposing you are not, if there is anything else in your neighborhood which is eatable. You rise up in sudden indignation and scare the committee away. In that case you have offended the coyote family deeply, and they retire to a safe distance and bark ceaselessly until they have hooted you out of the neighborhood. That night he and his companions will probably come and steal the straps from your saddle, the meat from the frying-pan, and politely clean the pan, and the boots from your bedside. Nothing that was originally derived from animal organization, or has the faintest flavor of grease, comes amiss to him. Through a thousand variations in his family history, the disposition to gnaw something remains unchanged. There is no more formidable array of ivory than his, and his greatest delight in life is ever to have something rancid between his teeth.

There is a distant collateral branch of this extensive family, which has for ages been noted for its cunning and rascality. The first beast with which a child becomes intimately acquainted is the fox. He has illustrated more pretty fables than all other beasts; he has beautified more picture books, and brought out more artistic skill. In reality he possesses but one advantage over the coyote, and that consists in his proverbial swiftness of foot. His brush is no larger and bushier, and his coat no thicker. Probably neither of these rivals in the science of stealing can lay any great claim to personal beauty, and considering his want of speed the coyote is the better beast of the two, in the particular line for which they are all distinguished.

In the great plains of the south-west, and the mountains of New Mexico, one is puzzled to know where a beast so wanting in ferocity and so slow of foot, can possibly obtain his daily meat. The truth is that he has to live by his wits. No one ever saw a starved coyote. He does not confine himself to any particular diet, and wherever he may wander or rest, he is evidently always thinking of his next meal. He would distinguish himself by stealing domestic fowls, only there are none in his dominion to steal. But he does not abandon his occupation on that account. He has the Chinaman's fancy for bird's nests, and he follows the mountain quail to her bundle of twigs, and daintily laps the inner sweets of a dozen eggs, and retires like a man from a free lunch, slily licking his chops. In the dead hours of the night he creeps upon the covey resting in the coarse grass, their tails together and their heads beneath their wings; even the wary old whistler who leads and guards his interesting family daily over the intricate miles of their *habitat* himself sound asleep; and throwing his sprawling fore-paws suddenly over as many as he can, leaves the rest to whirr screaming away in the darkness, and learn from him a useful lesson of family vigilance for the future.

The Jackass rabbit, doomed to fame, partly on account of swiftness, but mainly because of his grotesque auricular development, frequently falls a victim to the strategy of this marauder, at whom, under ordinary circumstances, he might be supposed to sit upon his hinder legs and derisively smile. Jack is sometimes so incautious as to be tempted by a damp and shady nook, to lie upon his back like a squirrel, and with his ears conveniently doubled under him, and his gaunt legs in the air, to too soundly sleep. Then the coyote creeps cautiously upon him, licking his lips, and as quiet as to voice as though he had never waked the lugubrious echoes. He may spend an hour in the task, and finally he makes a spring not the less rapid because it is awkward, and the poor rabbit takes his last lesson in gnawing subjectively.

The virtue of perseverance shines brightly in the coyote. All these things require an inexhaustible fund of patience. Of course he fails in many of his murderous attempts, but none the less does he try again. There is a notable instance in which this quality alone brings him victory, and that is in his contest with the buffalo. In this, since the supply of meat will necessarily be large, he makes common cause with all his hungry neighbors. The old bull, after many years of leadership, and after becoming the father of a horde of ungrateful descendants, is finally driven forth from the herd by the strong necks and ambition of his younger associates, and ruminates with two or three superanuated mates, while the herd wanders afar off forgetful. Then the coyotes take him in charge. Wherever he goes they hungrily follow. He dare not lie down, and weariness helps to overcome him. Finally they begin to harrass him openly and with increasing boldness. A gray assassin is upon every hand? The buffalo is too imperturbable a brute to ever succumb to mere barking, and his enemies begin to actually bite? The contest may last for many days, and be fought over a territory several miles in extent. The old monster is crippled and finally brought down, and a snarling feast is commenced, which continues until the last bone is picked bare.

But all the coyote's other modes of obtaining a livelihood are mere by-play to the great business of his life, which is stealing. For a long time it has been supposed that a cat approaching the cream-jar, and a weasel intent upon coveted eggs, were the ideals of sly cunning and predatory silence. But in the exhibition of a preternatural talent for silent appropriation, the coyote excells all the sharp-smelling and light-footed night-wanderers besides. He has a remarkable *penchant* for harness, rawhide and boots. He gnaws the twisted lariat from the pony's neck, and bodily drags away the saddle and chews it beyond recognition by the owner. He enters the open barrack-window and steals the accoutrements from the soldier's bed-post, and the shoes from beneath his pillow. He will walk backward and draw a dry raw-hide, hard and juiceless as a board, a mile from where he found it. It would seem that he did not steal these things for food alone. In the majority of cases they are beyond the mastication even of a coyote's restless jaws. He steals, as some men do, because he is a born criminal. He is largely gifted with the sense of smell, and the savory order of the camp-fire frying-pan reaches his appreciative olfactories a long way off. With drooping tail and lowered head he comes stealthily near like a thievish dog, and his appearance in the darkness is the very picture of treachery. He is patient, and will not be driven far, but crouches down a hundred yards away, and longingly licks his lips and waits. Then his brethren silently come, and ere long the little bright fire and the tired, lounging figures around it are surrounded by a cordon of patient, harmless, hungry thieves who lick their jaws and faintly whine in expectation.

These are the times, and only these, when the coyote is silent. Upon all other occasions his voice is his pride and glory, and he throws back his head in the ecstasy of discord, and gives it to the wind and the night in a rapid succession of discordant yelps, which seem ceaseless for hours together. Indeed, the coyote's bark is the prominent feature of night in the wilderness. To one unaccustomed to it, sleep is impossible. In spite of the knowledge of the brute's cowardice and general harmlessness, it is impossible to banish restlessness and some feeling of fear. After the fire dies out, as the sleepless and discordant hours pass, you long for morning and peace.

Coyotes and Indians are supposed to be on good terms always. They are somewhat alike in characteristics, and possess a mutuality of interests. They both object to the invasion of the white man, and both are cotemporary occupants of a country which cannot long remain the home of either. But the coyote's dislike to the invader is unreasonable, for he has been furnished more feasts upon the carcasses of causelessly slaughtered buffalo in one year than the Indian would have given him in ten.

But our gray-coated firiend makes a near approach to respectability in one item : he is a creature of family, for which he duly provides. Any morning in early spring, upon some dry knoll may be seen three or four little brown-colored, stupid-looking cubs, lazily enjoying the early warmth. At the slightest alarm they tumble with more alarcity than gracefulness into the mouth of the den, from which they never wander far, and many an hour's patient digging will not unearth them. Not far off may be seen the mother, uneasily watching the course of the intruder's footsteps. But provision for a family is not carried so far among the coyotes as it is in the fox family. There are no delicate morsels carried to the den, and the adolescent thief must subsist upon his mother's scanty udders until he has attained his teeth and his voice, when he is launched upon the wilderness world fully prepared by nature and instinct to practise all the variations in music and theft, and to follow in the devious ways of all his ancestors.

He is a brute which is entitled to respect from his very persistence and patience in knavery. Contemptible in person and countless in numbers, he forages fatness from things despised of all others. He is patient in his cunning, persevering in crime, and independent of all resources except his own. He is utterly careless of the contempt which all other beasts seem to have for him, waiting for his revenge for the time of their feebleness and decay. Like all cowards, he can fight desperately when he must, and the borderer's dogs wear many ugly scars of his making. Winter and summer, in heat and cold, he wags his way along the prairie-path with the same drooping, quick-turning watchful head; the same lolling red tongue, the same bushy tail trailing behind; ever mindful of a coyote's affairs, ever looking for supper; the figure-head, the feature, the representative of the broad and silent country of which he comes more nearly being master than any other.

THE PRIEST OF EL PASO.

THE town of El Paso del Norte is a bright dot in a green ribbon of fertility between frowning mountains. The green velvet ribbon is the valley of the Rio Grande, and El Paso is the jewel which lies upon it. Such is its description as set down in the chronicles of ancient times.

This important point in the Mexican empire was not young when Cincinnati was a hamlet and Saint Louis a French trading-post; Indiana a beech-grown wilderness and Illinois a wide and inhospitable jungle of tall grass. What though the Connestoga wagons carried the trade of the young city of William Penn to the valley of the Ohio, and the rich and waiting heart of a continent lay unheard-of and uncared-for, biding its time amid its silent forests and great rivers. The three generations that had lived and died in El Paso had not cared for nor even heard of these things. The priest in his gown and hat went his way in the streets, and the laden donkeys stood in the market-place. It was sunny then as now, and the rich grape-clusters ripened in the beams, and the wine-vats gave forth their ordors through court-yard doors as the blood-red juice ripened and grew rich within, and crept through chinks and grain-holes, and lay in odorous pools upon the floor. And the church was there as it is now. Just the same in its barbaric magnificence, only the huge cedar-beams of the roof were not then covered with a gray mould, and the central arch had not sunk and cracked until its key-stone hung perilously in its niche. The brown sand-stone slabs in the yard tell us all that, as we read in the ancient and half-defaced characters, of the Dons and Senoras who, in the odor of sancity, went to rest here A. D. 1798.

But of all things, and least of all, did these people suspect what their grandchildren should live to see. The Jeusit himself, the best judge of the course of empire and best prophet of political and social changes as he is, did not suspect that one day the boundaries of an infant Republic should widen until within gun-shot of his church and almost within the sound of his chant, and only upon the other shore of the river his brethren had discovered, named and claimed as their own, should arise a Yankee town, named after a great mechanic who was not less a genius and a sage, and that yet a little further and still within sight, should float in his own sunshine that silken, sheeny, starry thing, the emblem of free men and free faith.

We have said that it was seventy years ago. But the old man with whom the two strangers talked did not tell them of the changes between then and now. They were not in his thoughts, and not in the story he told. But his long white beard and silvery hair and shrunken limbs suggested it, and as he seated himself in the leathern-bottom chair, its cedar framework polished and black with age and use, they were the words he used as a beginning,—"Seventy years ago, Cabelleros,—seventy years?"

It was a curious chamber in which they sat. The walls were high and mouldy, and the cob-webbed ceiling was far up in shadow. The one tall window had lost all glass except a few of the lower panes, and the cotton cloth which supplied its place fluttered as the autumn nightwind wandered through. Through this window they had first seen the interior, for wandering through the rambling streets at midnight, one is curiously attracted by a light which dimly burns in the dilapidated window of an ancient church. Standing upon the grass-grown walk beside the wall there was no concealment of a figure upon whose shoulders lay the thin white hair, and who, prone upon the earthen floor stretched his attenuated arms toward the Mother of Sorrows in supplication, rigid, silent, pitiable. He was alone. The lamp smoked in its bracket upon the wall, and the small flame in the narrow fire-place served but to throw grotesque shadows through the narrow space. The star-lit darkness enfolded the old town in a shadowy cloak. Even the guitar was silent and the door-lights put out, and the far peaks of the mountains seemed to guard in the darkness a scene strange enough in noonday, and mediæval, sombre and mysterious at midnight beneath the stars.

They were strangers; it was their business to learn. Who could he be, who prayed so long and silently? Presently he rose up and passed out into the body of the church, and a moment afterwards the bell upon the gable rang a few sonorous strokes. At the sound in the stillness the sleeper may have turned in his bed and uttered his shortest prayer, and turned again to sleep. To go round and walk up the aisle of graves and stand in the ever-open door, was something which curiosity prompted and soon done. The old man stood there, the bell-rope still in his hand, cautiously listening. They could not tell if there was surprise in his eyes as they entered, but there was kindness in his action as he bade them wait where they stood. They heard his slow footsteps as he passed back through the darkness to the room where they had seen him first. Presently he came again, the lamp held above his head, peering through the gloom.

"Would you pray, Senors?" said he in the piping treble of age.

They told him they came not to pray but to talk. He hesitated a moment between doubt and courtesy, and then, bidding them follow, led the way over the hard earthen floor, past the altar-rail, at which he bent his decrepit knees, by images whose faces had a ghostly look in the dim lamplight, and into the room which seemed his chamber, and where they had seen him as he prayed.

He turned to them with a gesture which had in it a mixture of courtesy and irony, waved his hand around the apartment as who should say "here it is all,—look!" and seated himself in the one old chair and looked into the fire. The place had a faint mouldy smell, and that suggestion of quiet age which it is hard to describe. The earthen floor was worn until it was hard and smooth as stone. Upon one side were presses whose doors had parted from hinge and hasp, and whose panels dropped away piecemeal, and within them were glimpses of yellow linen and scarlet vestments and faded and tarnished lace. There was nothing there surely that was worth a question, and as the old sacristan,—for such seemed to be his office,—still sat with his back toward them looking intently at the glowing coals, they asked him none.

But in the midst of mouldiness and decay one comparatively small object attracted attention from its apparent freshness. Against the wall and immediately beneath a crucifix was a frame of dark wood some four feet long by one wide.

It shone with frequent polishing, and within it hung a

curtain of green cloth. It might have passed unnoticed save for the suggestion of concealment. They were there to see, and should they not know what lurked behind the small green curtain? It mattered little perhaps, but as one of them touched its corner with his finger the sacristan rose up with a polite deprecating gesture at which they stood ashamed. He took the lamp from its place and trimmed it afresh. Contrary to all expectation there was interest and pleasure in his eyes as he approached the panel with the lamp in his hand and tenderly raised the curtain. "Look," said he, "the hand that made it was a cunning one. He who painted those lines was a great artist,—one of the greatest of his times, but none will ever know it. In the old land across the sea are great paintings, and the names of their creators are immortal. But he whose hand made this was as great as they. He and they might have worked together, and you might now know who I mean. But no, you do not know,—you will never know. There were few who did, and they are dead. There is nothing left but this,—only this poor thing. Ah! he was a poet, an artist, rich and a grandee. He was handsome as a god and learned as a sage,—and this is all there is left, Senors,—there is nothing else."

Whatever opinion either of them had formed of the old man whose eyes had lighted with a new fire as he spoke, they were mistaken. He was not the peasant and churl they thought him, and no one need be mistaken who now saw the animated look in his keen old eyes his clearly-cut and handsome features, and the lithe figure which even in age seemed rather of the camp and the sword than of the bell and gown.

When one in the guise of a peasant descants upon art, the specimen named may certainly attract at least a passing moment's attention. The carefully-cared-for piece which filled the frame was vellum dried and horny with age, on which was traced in colors which had lost none of their brillancy, a Latin sentence. The head-letters had in them all the intricate and graceful beauty of the old art of illumination, and truly in intricacy of design, brilliancy of color and graceful detail the work was that of no unaccustomed or unskilled hand.

But as the stranger scanned the picture,—for picture it might really be called,—the words themselves seemed remarkable. There was a meaning and purpose in them: and in the position they occupied. The legend ran thus

ET NE ME INDUCES IN
TENTATIONEM,
SED LIBERA ME A MALO.

"Lead *me* not into temptation, but deliver me from evil." It was only a part of that form which is not so much a formula as a guide, which has been sent upward by millions of hearts for these eighteen hundred years, as the essence of prayerful hope. "Lead *me* not into temptation;" why were they written here?

"If these words have a history, father, and the man you speak of made them will you tell it to us?" asked one of them.

There are two conditions in which age delights; one in silence, the other extreme garrulity. The aged man, be he soldier, statesman or priest, lives mainly in the past. When silent he thinks, not of what he shall do and accomplish and *be*, as he did when he was young; but of what he *was* and remembers. When he talks he tells of those things, and either the condition of silence or discourse is his chiefest delight. And a smile crept into this wakeful old man's features again, as he heard the request. "Why not, my sons?" he said; and as he changed the title from Caballeros to" sons," he expressed the feeling of gratification which warmed his old heart. The strangers could guess by the commonest rules of that ill-learned lesson, life, that the sarcristan's heart clung to this spot and its story with a concentrated affection. A memory of something greater or grander or better, congenial to him through hope, affection or memory, rather than through actual experience, kept him near the spot.

"Why not, my sons? since there is ever something more in the commonest life, than appears upon the surface. My race is one that loves glory and art and beauty, but we love also God and the holy church. You are from the north and the blood in you veins is very cold. Your reformers,—the heretics who have led so many astray, and traduced and denied the Church which alone can save, throughout the world, were strong men here,"—and he touched his forehead,—"but they were cold *here*," placing his hand upon his heart. "You can understand your Luther and your Melanchthon and your Huss, but you cannot understand the gallant Knight of Pampeluna, brilliant in armor and flushed with glory, who founded the Society of Jesus ;—the sword *and* the cross,—your cold race can never understand *that.*" The sacristan had arisen as he spoke, and stretched forth his thin right arm as though he measured his antagonist's rapier.

"But the story, father," said one of them; "you forget the story."

The sacristan sank again into his chair, and the sadness

came again into his face. "The legend upon the wall reminds me of that," he said. "It was placed there seventy years ago. It is a long time, my sons — a very long time. The world has changed since then," and added, " else you would not be here. But I will speak, and afterwards you shall judge."

"Don Juan Amados was of a house which claimed a drop of the bluest blood in Spain. They stood ever near to greatness of lineage and greatness of deed. But Don Amados was the princeliest of them all, because God made him so. Shall I describe him to you, my sons? Then I will say again that you cannot understand him — he was not of *your* kind. He had an oval olive face, eyes that shone in kindness and flashed in anger, and the form and bearing of a soldier and a noble. How beautiful his hair was; so black and clustering, and how tender and strong his voice. He was the handsomest man in Spain! Men admired and respected him, and women loved him. He was as great in mind as he was beautiful in person. He was learned in all the learning of his time. The great universities of Spain could teach him no more, and last, he was a soldier. He could not have been otherwise. It is in his race, as I told you, to love the cross and the sword. I will not tell you, my sons, of how he fought in the wars of his country. I do not love to think of the old days of glory and strength. They sadden me. But I tell you that had my country remained as she once was; had her gallant sons begotten their like again, our holy church would ere this have been the church of the world. Ah, she had fallen before I was born — she was failing when Don Amados was a youth, but I know what she was;—God's will be done.

"But Don Amados loved not alone glory; he loved

the church, and when he was as young as either of you my sons, he became—a priest. Do you smile? Ah, *caramba*! Your cold race knows nothing either of glory or religion! I need not tell you how he became a priest; only that it was duty, love, *conscience!* Do you know what I mean by the last? No, you cannot even understand *that.* Well it was simply that Don Amados had sinned all the sins of noble youth, and in time he would purge them away and forget them.

"He asked of the council a mission, and they sent him here,—even here. It pleased him, for he knew not that Spain's daughters may be beautiful and frail everywhere· They are all dead now who remember the priest who came to the parish of El Paso del Norte from across the sea. But I have heard them tell of his noble face and his graceful bearing, which even the priest's garments might not conceal.

"You think he made a mistake; it is like your people to thus weigh and calculate. He did not. Many in our holy church have borne the pyx and chalice who could strongly wield the sword. Many times has the rosary hung in the rapier's place.

I told you in the beginning that he was a great artist. After he came here he was doubtless lonely, and his life much changed from what it had ever been before. So he beguiled the time with colors. In this very room he did it, and his easel sat there by the window, and this upon which I sit was his seat. At one time he painted the High Mass in the Barcelona cathedral. Then he made a head of the dead Christ, a morning at the Sepulchre and many smaller ones. They hung here and in another room, and there were many of them, for he labored rapidly and diligently. It was his life, his occupation. He did nothing but paint and pray. How beautiful they were, and how his soul was absorbed in them.

"The last painting he ever made was a Madonna. Not a sad and tearful Mother of Christ, but one whose features had in them a radiance and glory, not of faith and prophecy, but of human beauty. Ah, and the face was one which those who sleep yonder have told me they knew, and all El Paso knew. It was the gem of all, and a curtain hid it in its place, and those only saw it who chanced to catch a glimpse.

"By and by his soul was wrapped in art, and he almost forgot he was a priest. He knew he was forgetting, but while he did hard penance he still painted. He loved it; he was an artist, my sons, and could not help it.

"Once upon a time there came to El Paso a dignitary of our government, one who travelled in state, mighty in wisdom and in position. There accompanied him others, only less than he. Senor Otero came to this church, and scarce waiting to pray, passed on and entered this room. But he stopped in the midst and gazed. He called his companions and bade them also look. He was astonished and enraptured. Where is he who made these? he said. Bring him to me, for I would tell him something to his great good. And they that stood there said, it is only the padre Amados who did it. What? said he, the priest? I care not; he has that in him which should not rust here. Then the priest came, and the Senor Otero eyed him and saw his presence and his face. Father, said he, if thou wilt come with me, thou shalt have fame and gold, for truly thou art mistaken in thy calling. Wilt sell them? Name thy sum.

"Then Amados hung his head and turned pale, and when at last he had declined to sell, Senor Otero departed thinking strangely of the man, and wondering that priests were oft such geniuses and such fools; but, said he, thou shalt hear from me again ere long.

"On that same night the priest locked his door,—that very door, my sons,—and was for a long time alone. What he did, God knows,—His will be done,—but 'tis told how a great smoke arose from the chimney-top, and in the morning he lay here so prone in prayer, so wrapped in deep devotion that none dared disturb him. This that I tell you is indeed true, that pictures, canvas, colors and easel were here never seen again. The fire consumed them or the flood drowned them, and the priest came forth pale, sad and very silent, and went his ways and did his offices with a new humility. In a day following the few who ever entered here saw the panel in the wall. It was the last; he touched brush or canvas no more.

"But my sons, a man may pray full oft, 'Lead me not into temptation!'—he may write it in colors never so beautiful beneath his crucifix, and may cast away in the bitterness of self-sacrifice all he has himself made which may hinder him aught, and there will still be left one whose beauty he can neither make nor mar, and whom he cannot put away. I told you that the priest was lordly, learned and beautiful. I said he was also a scholar and a soldier. I may end by saying that he was also a man. He might burn his priceless Madonna, but the beautiful face which had crept into it, he could not destroy. It was there,—upon the street and at the open door. Do you know women, my sons? If you do, you are older than you look, and have learned most there is to know. This priest had defeated but the first temptation. He was accustomed to admiring eyes, for there are men from whom admiration is scarce concealed. The demi-gods are few, but this man was one. How might a priest come to know the startling fact that a woman loves him, and yet be innocent. Ah, there is no tale-bearer who delivers his message so easily as a woman's eyes and a woman's rosy cheek. The Dona Anita did not admire the glorious priest, she did not even love him,—she adored him. She was not a maniac, in any greater sense than many have been since Adam. But the mass had come to be a ceremonial not for her soul but for her heart; not for God, but for the priest who officiated. Think you, I am telling a strange thing? Doubtless, for your race is not as ours; you are *very* cold. But she did not bring her love and lay it at his feet. Women are born with a better knowledge of men than that. Yet there is no land to which she would not have followed him afar off, no fortune which she would not have shared. Yet without hope, since he was a priest.

"But I said he was a man, and he knew all this. Nay, it was not that which troubled him; it was the other fact that he carried in his heart the image of the Dona Anita. The Madonna's face was also her face, and perchance she had heard as much. He met her on the street, and a thrill went to his heart when his gown but touched her garments. He saw her beautiful face as she knelt at the altar-rail, and, (God pardon him,) he could have dropped the Host and fled away from his duty and his vows. You know that this priest was a heroic man, and was a priest for conscience' sake, and for that cause had abandoned that only one other thing which is dearer than love—fame. Those who knew have told me that from vesper-bells to matin, he lay all night upon this floor and prayed to be delivered. He was wan and worn with

penance and fasting, and yet, perchance between his eyes
and the face of the blessed Mother as he prayed, came
that other warm human face clothed with a nearer love.
"You think as you listen, that there can be little more
to a story like this. But I am old; it pleases me to tell
all, and you will listen. It came about by and by, that
the priest and the Dona understood each other, and while
she disguised less and less as she drew nearer to him
across the great impossibility, so grew more and more
upon him the irksomeness of his holy office. Yet they
dared not speak, scarce even look, the one to the other.
There have been many battles fought in men's souls,—
harder and more costly than the battles of kings. This
man knew how to fight, and had conquered once. But
he was beleagured now indeed, for he loved his enemy.

"One night, in this room, the priest thought he was
alone. He walked back and forth, not quiet and calm,
but flushed, anxious and almost despairing. As he passed
by, his shadow fell again and again upon the window,
and one there was near who saw it each time. There
are times, I am sure, when even priests, being men, lose
faith in penance and prayer. This may have been to
him one of those times. By and by she who looked at
the window knew that he stopped opposite to it and
stood still. Then there was the quick movement of
systematic action, the faint clink of metal, and finally
when the outer door was opened, there stood at the
threshold a figure in plumed helmet, the baldric upon
his breast, and the bright scabbard upon his thigh. The
lamp-light shone upon him as he looked about him,
unconscious of a spectator. Ah, my sons, it was not
altogether boyish. In thinking and longing, doubting
and loving, can we wonder that he longed once more to

know the feel of the sword—the sensation of a far-gone life? The best of us do much we would not wish the world to smile at, and a soldier may not be blamed if he hides among a poor priest's effects the plume that has waved in purple smoke, and the sword he has drawn in the service of his country!

"If you and I were women, we might know how she felt, who watched him then. No more a priest? Ah, how natural to forget the reality and see only the sham. Slowly she came toward him, and as she drew near where he stood he saw her. He was fastened to the spot in his dream of temptation. She came very close and seated herself,—nay, kneeled, at his feet. 'Tis an old story; as she kissed his passive hand perhaps he could look down into the beautiful eyes. Women are not slaves, neither are their lovers, but sometimes they dispute who shall be the humblest. The town was asleep as it is to-night. The priest forgot himself in the soldier and the man, and he stooped and kissed again, not her hand,—the first woman's hand that had touched his for years,—but her very lips.

"Men are the same everywhere, and the priest remained a priest until the Sabbath morning. High mass came again. We go not so far as to tell of men's hearts. Even if his offices in the high altar of holy church were heartless, many men's have been so ere now. We cannot tell. But the Dona Anita came and knelt at the altar-rail. The priest gave to her that which is the body of Christ. No wonder that as he saw her face, the flood which is without volume or sound, and which none see, overwhelmed him. He dropped the chalice from his hand, and tore the robe from his shoulders, and coming down from his place, passed out through the startled people, through the open door, and hastened away from his office, from the bosom of the holy church, from conscience, honor and hope, forever. The legend was written in vain, and it stands in its place only to remind us, all, my sons, that love may conquer, where fame and glory and wealth shall be beaten in the contest."

The old sacristan arose and took the lamp again from the bracket, and bowed toward the strangers. When past the altar and the images, and through the shadows they again reached the open door, the wierd hour of early morning was upon the world. The old man stood in the passage, and the light wind played with his long gray hair, and the lamp-light glanced upon his thin and sharply outlined features, as he bade them farewell. The man was remarkable as his story, and one of his guests turned before he departed for one more word.

"Father," said he, "we express our thanks, but will you not tell us who you are?"

"Others could tell that my son, would you but inquire; but you are strangers. My name is mine only by inheritance and not by baptism. Men call me Garcia, for so the church has named me, but my father was a soldier and a nobleman and I disclaim him not. I am the son of Don Juan Amados, he for whose soul I nightly pray, and my mother sleeps in the last place but one, on the right hand as you go out. God go with you." And the old sacristan turned and went back among the memories and shadows.

LA SENORITA.

IF a person of the masculine profession,—we use the word advisedly,—invades that territory which is set apart and occupied by the tastes, ideas and fashions of the fairer sex, he is immediately accused of having seen all that he afterwards goes and writes about through a mere crevice in the armor of predjudice similar to the peep-hole in turret of a monitor. But no one need be deterred by stinging missiles fired at him with astonishing rapidity, but which he knows were never intended for the infliction of a mortal wound. And the fair-haired descendants of Norman knights and Saxon thanes need feather no darts upon this occasion. They may well continue the fashioning of basques and the comparison of braids, and the silent but none the less entertaining communion with the mirror, for there is a woman whose characteristics are controlled rather by race than education, graceful and coquettish rather by nature than design, and so far away that in these climes her olive face is never seen. She could not read this if she would, and it is her of whom we write.

The Spanish woman,—for she is intensely Spanish still,—comes upon the traveller very unexpectedly as he journeys toward the south-west. In the old monotony of the plains, and the newer and not less wearisome sameness of the mountains, he has perhance almost forgotten the airiness of calico and the flutter of ribbons. Squaws he has perhaps seen; evil-faced slaves who are female merely, not womanly. In the curious aspect of the first Mexican town, he sees a life around him which it is impossible to have anticipated. There is the little house, white-washed and garnished, and troubled with an eruption of brown spots; shaded with pear trees and nestled in the midst of a sunny door-yard scene which teaches him that poverty is no bar to content. He sees the herds of goats and the solemn procession of laden asses, and every evidence of a life which is alone among the mountains of a far country, and which imitates and cares for no other life.

It will be strange, if he sees not first and last and remembers longest among those things, a creature who also watches him with less of curiosity than sly coquettishness in very black eyes. But persons and places, and even distinct and curious phases of character, have but a trival and fleeting interest unless connected with certain associations. It is not the mere romantic idea, which causes one to recogonize in this nut-brown woman the representative in America of the peasant woman, perchance the high-born Dona, of that old country whose cross-emblazoned flag has been borne to the ends of the earth, leaving ever behind it a trail of desolation. It was beneath that flag that the Spanish woman became American, in the old time of strength and conquest, and unchanged in manner, appearance or taste she still remains, rendered by circumstances which surround her a still more remarkable woman than the borderer's wife, who in time to come will occupy the house across the way, and be jealous of her vivacious neighbor.

The life of the border changes all men and women into people of its own kind, and makes them anew for its purposes; all except the Senorita. The pretty, oval face, the bright black eyes, the careless laugh and the tongue especially trained by race and habit to the glib utterance of a torrent of oily sentences, are here unchanged in the lapse of two centuries. To the Spanish woman there is no frontier, because she is ignorant of any other country. The frontier is an American institution, and she and her male companion lack the instinct of immigration. What to us is new, to them is old beyond memory. Here has ever been the church, the padre, the guitar, the fandango, the gossipping neighbor, the cigarette, and these are all there is of life. Yet the Senorita is not an uneducated woman. Tradition is her teacher. The world wonders that the Spanish mind cannot change at home, but it has not changed even here. No people, not even the Jews, show more perfectly the effects of concentrated nationality. Yet this woman has a weakness for the Yankee which is the bane and torture of her husband's and her lover's life. She smiles upon him in health and comforts him in misfortune. She will follow him wherever he may wander throughout their rugged country. But through all she will cling to her church, her language and her race, and finally return to her native village, by no means forsaken by her family, with the same loving smiles for the coming man.

The Senorita's very vices are not hers in any extraordinary sense, but are in accordance with the Latin idea of virtue. What shocks the Anglo-Saxon, what renders her an outcast utterly abandoned and forsaken, is to this woman the coolest matter of course. With a character which the queen of the *demi-monde* would declare was none of hers, the Spanish woman is chaste in dress, language and deportment, beyond her education and her surroundings. Those little offenses, which seem scarcely to interfere with connubial felicity or motherly duties, she groups under the general name of love. Her faithfulness is to be faithful to but one at once, but that one is seldom her husband. Him she has of course, and him she keeps. Her church holds that marriage is a sacrament and not a contract. Divorces and permanent separations are almost unknown. The elderly Spanish woman, her youthful sins forgotten or classed among the incidents consequent to beauty, generally has about her a brood of children, and is as matronly and faithful in their care as was her lamented grandmother before her. Such a condition of society as this, it is hard to describe with any hope of being believed. There is no apparent debauchery, no proclamation of brazen vice in word or manner, no lack of delicacy or courtesy, no rupture of the visible peace of families or the routine of domestic life, and yet chastity, as a virtue, even as a name, is nearly unknown.

In contradistinction, though not in denial of all this, a large part of the Senorita's life is taken up in the exercise of the forms of religion. Her village is indeed a poor one, if it has not a church more or less ancient in the midst of the plaza. There, at all times of the day she and her devotional companions kneel a-row, and patter their prayers in a language they never hope to understand, and with a glibness of tongue and vacancy of face which reminds one of children learning a spelling-task. She may nod and smile at an acquaintance who brings with him a reminiscence of last night's fandango; she will undoubtedly see and hear all that passes within the wide range of a woman's curiosity, but for her soul's sake she pauses no instant in her monotonous devotions. She is constant at the confessional, where it may reasonably be doubted whether amours are considered sins, else she would spend her life in penance.

This startling combination of religious devotion and social crime, necessarily occupies a large place in the recollections of this unique female, remembered too, by comparison with those with whom she has little in common. But in a country where character and life take strange phases in all respects, the most unaccustomed contradictions in manners and morals soon cease to attract particular attention. These things come far short of being the sum of all the oddities of the Senorita. There is probably no woman within the bounds of civilization, who may be called a fair representative of her race; in other words, who is as bad as the males of her own kind. The Mexican farmer is a plodding, dark-faced, surly and silent creature, wanting alike in ambition and force, loving sunshine, idleness and cigarettas with the only devotion his nature knows. He dances the blithe measures of the fandango with a face that indicates, if anything, only the solemn performance of a duty. He is lazy even in the midst of the vivacious conversation of his race. Gesticulating, shrugging, frowning and stamping, there is still a perceptible indolence in the pantomime. The smooth syllables of his mother-tongue were contrived for ease rather than force. Sober he is stupid; drunk he is simply surly. There is an immense deal of character in intoxication. The Indian screams and dances, and is possessed with a mania for the infliction of outrages upon defenseless creatures. The Irishman longs for a new experience of that delicious sensation consequent upon the breaking of a head. The German laughs mostly; and the Yankee does anything which it enters his erratic head to do. Now the Spaniard sits silent and broods upon the wrongs he has suffered during the whole of his aimless life, and meditates revenge.

Drunkenness develops his national instinct of stealth. If under the influence of *aguadiente* he can accomplish an adroit stab in the back, or a shot from behind a wayside rock, he will have accomplished the brightest of his drunken dreams.

In these things the woman is his opposite. She it is who furnishes the element of cheerfulness in a land where but for the sunshine, nature herself would wear a perpetual frown. She is lithe, graceful, cheerful and kind-hearted. She delights in bright colors and gaudy scarfs, and knows full well the charm there is in the contrast between teeth that are white and eyes that are very black. With her, smiles and words are inseparably connected, and she makes no blunders in the distribution of either. Every question is politely answered, every salutation is gracefully returned. The water from the spring and the seat by the door are given with the same courtliness to all who ask, and with an utter contradiction of all the rules of sensibility, her brown cheek tinges with a blush which would become the modesty of a country bride. America is the only land which possesses that life which produces a class unique in the history of character. All the women of the border partake largely of their surroundings, and are ignorant, awkward and discourteous in direct proportion to their isolation,—all except the Senorita. Lacking totally all the sterling qualities of her white-haired and blue-eyed sister, she lacks also her awkwardness. It is in the race. The sturdy conquerors of the wilderness came not from the south. They have need only of strength.

In the Mexican woman there is a curious suggestion of something oriental. There is a sinuous grace of movement, a lazy contentment with surroundings, a perfect confidence in the apparent philosophy of life, and an unwavering faith in the perfection and completeness of her religious belief. Her domestic surroundings are such as she would have them, and she knows of no better. There is no more complete domestic system than hers, and she is thoroughly proficient in all the arts of home life. In her house there are no chairs, no closets, no stoves, no tin utensils and no soap. Her feats of cookery are performed in porous earthen basins, and the *frijoles* steam and bubble in a corner of the narrow hearth for two days. She makes bread, white and beautiful, without yeast or the bicarbonate nuisance. Her mattress is of wool, her rug a sheep-skin, her bed often a bank of earth against the wall, and she is ignorant of the use of that babyish luxury, a rocking-chair. When she smiles and says "*sientise, Senor*," she means that you should do that which an Anglo-Saxon never accomplished with any satisfaction to himself, namely, sit or lie upon a mat. Her ideas in the matter of dress are peculiar. So that her head, and the greater part of her face be concealed, it matters little for bust, arms and ankles. In two hundred years she has not forgotten the use of the scarf. It is her indispensable adornment. Bonnet and hat are not in her vocabulary, of stays she is utterly ignorant, and a high-heeled shoe she never saw; and yet this creature is a civilized woman. She affects ribbons, and in the matter of colors is the original Dolly Varden. She has a care for her complexion, and in the earlier hours of the morning may sometimes be caught with her face hideously encrusted with white clay. The dance is her passion, and her ear is ever alert to the thin strains of the guitar. The festive hall is splendid with strips of red calico, and brilliant with tallow-dips. The equipages which stop the way are not especially magnificent, being only a stupid assemblage of donkeys. Three of the belles of the ball can find place upon the back of a single one, and she is indeed aristocratic who has an animal to herself and some one to lead him in state through the rambling street.

The Senorita lacks none of the essentials of common decency, in the conduct of her domestic affairs. Her hearth is neat, her cookery savory, and her garments as white as snow. She is a careful housewife, as her husband is a careful farmer, and her sole extravagance is in the way of personal adornment. To look pretty is as much the constant endeavor of this isolated woman, as it is that of the frequenter of the opera, or the wallflower at a state reception. She is an arrant and incurable coquette, and often combines with all her feminine trickery a beauty which by no means suffers when compared with that of those accustomed to more aristocratic masculine worship.

The celebrated female known as the "peasant-girl," which the story-tellers and sketch-writers have used with such telling effect, has her home, as far as most of us know, in the vineyards of southern France, the hills of Normandy or the valleys of Switzerland. Surely no one has lighted upon such a creature anywhere in the United States. But she is here. You may see her at the door by the roadside any morning. She stands at the great gate of the *hacienda* as you pass, and would fain sell you eggs and goat's milk. You see her watching the goats and donkeys in the glades, or carrying water from the spring upon her head. We will not say of her what is unfortunately true of her elder sisters, and pleasantly remember her as the redeeming member of her race and family. She is but a developed child, simple, picturesque, content. She stands alone among the children of the frontier as one whose face is not chalky and freckled, whose limbs are not attenuated and whose hair is not white. Her feet are bare in the grass, and the two long braids of black hair are as yet unconcealed by the odious *rebosa*. She wears only a short skirt and that other intimate vesture of white texture and scant pattern, so well-known and so seldom mentioned. But she is unconscious of any possible want of further covering. It is a unique combination of innocence and traffic, for the gathered skirt is full of eggs, and she pipes as you pass: " *'wavas Senor,—mucho fresco!*" She laughs as she says it. It is her normal condition to be merry, and as you pass on, the most sour and sober of a sour and sober race could scarce be blamed for his recollection of a brown and comely face, round limbs, unspoiled innocence, and a pretty mouthful of teeth which shine in a habitual smile.

It were well that this picture of Mexican life might remain unchanged, and that the haggard woman of forty everywhere seen with no trace of the innocence of youth in her face, could have come to what she is only through hardship and natural decay. No one needs to be informed that if affairs go on as they now are, there will soon be no descendant of the Spaniard on this side the water to describe. It would seem that the decay of his race was fallen upon him, far distant among the mountains of a conquered province. Daily it is growing harder to believe what is nevertheless true, that the Senorita of New Mexico is the direct descendant of those dames which have played no inconsiderable part in the history of glory and the loves of kings. Sadly fallen indeed, both at

home and here, are the daughters] of a land from which
sprung Isabella and Catherine, Cervantes and Loyola:
the land to whose soil the crusader and the Jesuit are
alike indigenous; where Philip reigned and the Inquisition flourished, and whose conquests have marked the
new world with an indelible stain alike of power and
avarice, and nurtured for centuries an equal and commingled growth of religion and debauchery.

PEG.

"GIT outen hyar, Peg Watkins! Ef I come thar to you, I'll—," and there was a sound as of a broom alighting upon the brushy end, and the handle thereof striking the outer wall with a vigorous *thwack*.

"Now, in the name of wonder, who can this much-berated female be," mused the Doctor, as he heard the words and their accompanying emphasis. The doctor was the latest arrival. He was strange to the post and all its surroundings, having, only six weeks before, entered into a solemn contract with the high and mighty Medical Director, in the city of Philadelphia, to do duty as Acting Assistant Surgeon, U. S. A., at any post to which he might be ordered, and to regularly receive therefor the compensation of one hundred and twenty-five dollars per month, quarters and a ration. The doctor was not in delicate health, and did not think that the frontier might restore a shattered constitution. This was what most of his kind reported of themselves, together with other details of an extensive practice and influential connections, and the regrets which naturally fill a sensitive man's mind under such circumstances. But the brusk, sunburned fellows who were to be his associates had known many acting assistant surgeons in the same circumstances, and were not to be imposed upon. A new doctor means to the officers of a frontier post a something out of which a considerable amount of fun, some hospital brandy and some service is hereafter to be had, and he is welcomed and treated accordingly.

When the doctor had alighted from the ambulance, three days before, his appearance was as startling in these solitudes as though he had just escaped from another world—which, in fact, he in some sense had. He was dressed in grey cassimeres, an English walking-coat, and, to crown all, a tall white hat of the "plug" kind, deeply and solemnly bound with black. The air of Chestnut Street and the Continental Hotel seemed to emanate from him, as he stood there looking through the inevitable spectacles at the curious place which was, for an unknown time, to be his home. A group of swaggering fellows, all clad in blue, and each wearing the emblem of some military grade upon his shoulder, sauntered towards him from the trader's store. "Look at Pills," said one; "See that tile," remarked a second; "Bad health—large practice," remarked a third, epitomizing the usual story. But they ceased to laugh as they came nearer, and greeted him with that solemn courtesy which is the usual result of mistaken calculations with regard to an expected associate, dissipated at first sight. As those kind-hearted and careless fellows shook hands with "Pills," one by one, the prospect for "fun" out of a greenhorn did not seem a very brilliant one. The new doctor was a kind of blonde Nazarite, whose face, it seemed, had never known razor. He was so large that the men around him looked up into his open eyes, and felt for a minute afterwards the impression of a hand that was anything but velvet. "Bad health," remarked Thomson to his companions, shortly after: "bad health be d—d."

With the air of a man to whom nothing is strange which time and circumstances bring about, the doctor sat oiling his gun when the broom was thrown at Peg Watkins. The voice and the weapon, he knew, were the especial property of the octoroon who did the culinary offices of the mess. But having been here but three days, he might not have seen all the females of the post. So, with the reflection mentioned, he rose and walked to the door in expectation of seeing this creature, who had apparently been stealing something, make a hasty exit from the rear of the premises. What he did see was this: an immense yellow-and-white dog, who, with her bristles standing like a roach along her back, her head turned aside with that curious pretence of looking the other way which angry canines are apt to practise, and the pendent lip drawn away from her wide, square jaws, displayed a glittering phalanx of ivory to some antagonist at the kitchen door. Then this was the trespasser. The doctor laughed as he thought of it; Peg was only a dog.

But he was one of those men who have an extensive acquaintance among the hairy beasts who, in all ages and races, have chosen to be spurned, beaten, misunderstood and murdered as the friends and humble followers of man, rather than to live in savage independence without him. As he watched her with an amused expression in his face, it seemed to him that the shaggy creature was one who possessed more than ordinary share of canine character. "Come here, Peg; come, old girl," said he, and held out his hand. Peg was visibly disconcerted, and lowered her bristles, and looked astonished at hearing her name called in a tone of kindness. Then she crept humbly towards her new friend, and when she felt the touch of his hand, fairly grovelled in the dust before him, and finally followed him into the house. For months she had been assailed by missiles and epithets, whenever her shaggy form appeared in a doorway, and had stolen from the butcher and the garbage-barrel all she ate; and through it all, she had lain in front of the sally-port every night, watching and listening, the most vigilant sentinel of the command. She was an outcast, utterly abandoned, and only through inadvertence permitted to live. As she crouched close beside the walls, with forlorn countenance, and haggard, watchful eye, it seemed, had any cared to notice, that she felt, with such a feeling as her human masters often want, her utter ignominy and disgrace. Now, in less than two hours after her acquaintance with him, she lay in the twilight at the doctor's door with self-conscious importance, and disputed the entrance of the commandant himself. So are dogs—and men—wont to forget themselves upon a sudden change of fortune.

There is a road, a monotonous and desolate line across the desert, which leads westward from the Rio Grande. Over this have passed hundreds who never reached the end, and thousands who, if they did, never cared to return. Over plateaux where the tall cacti stand like ghosts, through canons Indian-haunted and lined with graves and crosses, the brown track stretches for hundreds of lonesome miles. But it is not wanting in travel. Here, through the long summer, the thousands of long-horned, thirsty Texas cattle drag their gaunt limbs along on the journey to California. Here is the man whose destiny it is to wander from place to place through life unsatisfied, surrounded by his dozen white-haired and boggle-eyed urchins, who probably were born by the roadside, and ever accompanied by the woman whose troubles are cured by a cob pipe, and whose amazing fecundity seems no hinderance to emigration. Sometimes, too, there are those who have a definite and more thoughtful purpose in wandering, and who run away from family difficulties, mothers-in-law and old associations. But to all, California is still the land of gold, and all underestimate beforehand the length and the peril of the road and the hard facts which lie at the end. But thus, for some inscrutable purpose directed by Providence, do Southern Arkansas, Texas and others of the Southern States empty themselves of their unstable population.

Some months before the doctor's arrival, several families of such had camped at the spring, whose semi-circular disc of stone opened the tepid water to light, a few hundred yards from the southern wall. The circumstance was not an unusual one, and would have attracted no attention had not the party stayed so long, and possessed some unusual attractions. They wanted an escort of soldiers, and waited until the return of a scouting party, so that the troops might be spared them. The men were well-dressed and independent, and the women were some of them comely, and all of them exclusive. There was one tall girl who attracted universal attention, as well on account of her beauty as her exclusiveness, who turned a cold eye upon Thomson himself, who in his day had been (the world of a soldier must be taken in this matter,) a famous woman-tamer. Tuck, the butcher's man,—"contractor's agent" he designated himself,—had, with cosmopolitan impudence, visited the new-comers' camp the first evening, and straightway fallen desperately in love with this young woman, and would have been willing to have been married to her then and there under a cottonwood by the post-adjutant, only that when he ventured upon a conversation with her she not only failed to reply, but puckered her pretty face and questioned of the man who seemed to be her father if they had not unfortunately camped in the vicinity of the slaughter-pen. Miss Margaret, the rest of them called her, and though thereafter Tuck called her "stuck-up," he nevertheless worshipped Miss Margaret from afar. She "didn't do nothin'," he said, and he noticed that when she was not reading a book whose binding suggested a different kind of literature from that to which he was accustomed, she sat apart, with her white hands in her lap, and looked very unhappy indeed.

By and by it was suspected that Miss Margaret held no relationship, unless a very distant one, to any of the party. The gallant and polite officers of the post were treated by her with some consideration, and they made, or suspected at least, this discovery. Thomson averred that she was a well-educated Northern girl, one of his own kind, who had gone South as a school-mistress, and been jilted by some person to the said Thomson unknown. He acknowledged that she had not told him so, or in any way given him her confidence. But the acute Thomson guessed it; and by George! it was a shame. When asked politely if she intended making a residence in far-off California, she said she did not know, and hinted that she did not care. The longer the party stayed, the more imminent became the prospect of a sensation of some kind, on account of a fair-haired and blue-eyed young woman who had captivated all hands, down to the butcher's-man. There had never been in these parts a sojourner upon the longest and most desolate road in the world, whose footsteps were so dainty, who wore white skirts and collars, and who coiled her yellow hair with such feminine grace upon a shapely head. But she was strange. She was in a sense homeless among her companions. Disregarding the apparent danger, she took long walks alone, and Tuck stated long afterwards that he once saw her far down towards the canon, sitting upon a boulder in the moonlight, apparently "thinkin'," and that beside her, alert and watchful, sat her sole companion upon such occasions, an ugly, yellow dog, who had always seemed to have an especial dislike to the contractor's agent.

One night after "tattoo," the man with whose family Miss Margaret seemed to be connected, came breathless to the commandant, with the statement that she had "gone walkin'" early in the evening, and had not returned. Nor did she ever return. The most accomplished trailer of the post failed to account for the direct means of her taking off. After a day and a night of fruitless search, all efforts were abandoned as useless,— as indeed they seemed to be, without a track through pathless wildness,—and thereafter the very theme was avoided, as a horrible reminiscence whose every detail was expressed by the one fateful, whispered word, "Apaches."

But was it accounted for by that word? Had her darkling walks ended in sudden capture and a fate worse than death? Mariano said not, and he knew. The scout declared that there had not been an Indian near the emigrant's camp, nor between there and the canon for three moons. Men would sometimes arrive at conclusions more nearly correct if they would study probabilities less, and improbabilities more. If the commandant had been asked if there was any other means by which Miss Margaret could have been spirited away, he would have said unhesitatingly, no. And yet there was. Every Friday night, at an hour when the wilderness itself seemed asleep, there came rattling down the hill from the eastward, a canvas-covered vehicle drawn by four vicious little mules. The officer of the day often heard its driver's coyote-bark, by which he roused the sleepy denizens of the trader's store, as he approached. The sentinel, as he walked back and forth before the sally-port, watched it as it paused for a moment at the door, and heard the leathern mail-bag fall upon the gravel. A sleepy word or two between the driver and the trader's clerk, the shutting of a door, the renewed grinding of wheels, and the overland stage had come and gone so quickly in the darkness that it seemed doubtful when daylight came if such an institution existed. Sometimes there were passengers, but not often. Occasionally a desperate man whose absolute necessities called him across a continent, loaded himself with weapons, and ran the gauntlet of danger in the " Overland." People wondered sometimes, why or how the line was run at all. The doubt was hardly a pertinent one. Some hundreds of thousands of dollars for a weekly mail-service, coupled with a contract that the coach must carry passengers, will accomplish wonders.

The old man who reported Miss Margaret's taking off to the commandant, confessed that she was not related to him or to his family; that she became connected with them in Eastern Texas, by being a teacher in his neighborhood. She had means, he said, was "offish an' book-larned," had started with them to California because she seemed to have some concealed purpose in going, and added that "she never tuk to him or his family much, and war a leetle quare in her ways." He probably forgot to state that on the night of her departure she had told the whole party distinctly that they would, in her opinion, never see California, and in terse and elegant terms, expressed her opinion of the slowness of

Texans in general, and these in particular. He also failed to state that she had taken a travelling-bag, but left behind an immense trunk, which, with all its unknown finery, might be regarded as a legacy to his carrot-headed daughters. In fine, Miss Margaret's guardian lied. The next day the emigrant party left the post, going westward.

More than a week after these things had occurred, and the tender hearts of the gallant gentlemen of the garrison had settled down to subdued regretfulness for Miss Margaret's supposed fate, as Tuck was plying his avocation at the slaughter-pen in the early morning, he was startled by the apparition of an immense yellow-and-white mastiff, gaunt, haggard and nearly starved, who came crouching towards him, urged by hunger, mutely begging for a bare smell of the fresh meat in which the churl was at work. He stopped, astonished, for he had no great difficulty in recognizing Miss Margaret's surly guardian. He stood with his bloody hands upon his hips, and as he looked he conceived a new hatred for the beast for her mistress' sake. "*You* kin come back, kin you? Drat yer ugly eyes," and he threw a stone at her. The poor creature yelped and limped away towards the post, too sore, tired and hungry to even show her teeth to the other beast who would, in the midst of food, deny a useless bone to a starving dog. When he saw her again he said, "There goes that Peg." This was cunning irony on the part of the brilliant Tuck, and he laughed loudly and hoarsely at the thought that the friendless dog should hereafter bear the nickname of her lost mistress. Then, because the name of Miss Margaret's protector was understood to have been Watkins, the servant girl, with something of the drollery peculiar to her race, had called her "Peg Watkins" the evening she became the doctor's friend.

As time passed the doctor dissipated all the theories upon which the officers of the post had based their pre-conclusions as to what, as a " contract doctor," he ought to be, and confirmed the impression he had given upon first sight. He accommodated himself to surroundings which might well be considered curious, in an hour's time. He had travelled much, knew men very well, and was cool in all emergencies. He was not afraid of sun or rain, was a keen hunter and an excellent companion, and could tell stories like Othello himself. He knew the miner in California, the ranchman in Texas, and was equally at home in Paris or Vienna. His companions respected him at first, and afterwards liked him well. As a physician, he was careful, bold, and gentle as a woman. But there was something about the man that, after all, they could not understand. Thomson remarked that he never talked of women in any way, and although the very kind of man, the gallant lieutenant thought, who was apt to have large experience in that line, he had no past flirtations to detail to his auditors. One night, soon after his arrival, the presence of the outcast mastiff at his feet, suggested the story of Miss Margaret. He only said, "Eh! Margaret?" and relapsed into thoughtful silence. In other respects he was strange, and like many men of his kind, lived largely within himself. He was always content, and even pleased to be alone. Often, accompanied by Peg, he passed the sentinel at midnight, coming in from some purposeless wandering. He was not unaccustomed to the life of the frontier. Only a year ago he had left California, and within a few months had been in Texas. He did not state the object of his wanderings but his conversation left the impression upon his auditors that he was either running away from or chasing an indefinite object around the world. Often, far in the night, when the officer of the day in his round passed the doctor's window, he could see the lonely gentleman sitting in the flickering candle-light, and Peg crouched watchfully in the open window. "Come here, Margaret, old girl," he could hear him say, and the surly dog would indulge in clumsy demonstrations of joy, and placing her huge paws upon the doctor's breast, thrust her square muzzle into his very beard. Her master was not a disciple of Tuck's, and in the matter of nicknames thought proper to reverse the matter, and that was all.

The understanding between the brute and the man was so remarkable as to attract considerable attention. Wherever the doctor's footsteps led him, the dog awkwardly waddled behind. Peg was now clean, well-fed, and carried her content to the extreme of being somewhat saucy. Her master was her universe, and she cared for nothing and no one else. The denizens of the post might pat her on the head if they would, and she reciprocated by hardly so much as the wagging of her tail. Hundreds of times her name was called from open doors, and across the parade-ground. She simply turned her head in careless inquiry, and walked slowly in the opposite direction. All this may have been a kind of dignified revenge for past indignities, for she had the general good at heart. Often in the watches of the night her bark came back from the hills sounding like a human halloo. There was a legend that she never slept. But she did—at mid-day, on the doctor's bed.

The saying that "time at last makes all things even" is only poetry, which is generally far from true. But there was a notable instance in which the axiom was demonstrated. Tuck possessed two curs as ugly as himself, one of which was of Peg's own sex. Early one morning, as he went to his avocation, they three met Peg walking with great dignity beside the wall. With his dogs behind him, Tuck could not resist the temptation to utter a vicious "sick 'm." With much more valor than judgment the butcher's dogs rushed to the onset. If Peg was frightened she made no sign of it, and dealing with one antagonist at a time, quietly took the female by the neck, and with one great shake covered her white breast with her enemy's blood. A few minutes after she walked quietly into the room where her master sat, apparently unconscious of the stain. Afterwards, when told of the outrage by Tuck, the doctor called his grim friend to him, and as he petted her remarked, "Peg, did you kill the meat-man's dog, eh?" And the "meat-man" went away, convinced that dogs and men may sometimes have a mysterious mutuality of interest.

The months of summer passed and autumn came, with its nights of frosty sparkle and moonlit glory. The walled post, with its bare parade-ground and its monotonous routine, dulled still more by daily use, grew irksome to the doctor. No wonder that he liked better to wander through the long brilliant evenings among the near foot-hills, accompanied always by Peg. His companions had long since grown used to his vagaries, and paid small heed to his absence, while they whiled the dull night away with friendly poker. True, they had concluded long ago that there "was something on the man's mind," and guessed, with how much truth they then little knew, that the position of "contract doctor" at a frontier post was, to a man of his attainments, little more than an excuse to get away from himself.

One night he lay upon his back by the roadside, a gaunt cactus lifting its thin spire at his feet, and Peg beside him, looking at the stars. His thoughts were dreamy, but they were busy. This refuge in the wilderness was not satisfactory. Go where he would he could not rid himself of a thought which had been with him so long that it was a part of himself. He had lain there three hours, and in that time had evolved another indefinite idea in regard to his further wanderings. Privately he had already resigned his appointment, and questioned where he should go. "If I could only find her," he said as he rose up, "I would start for China."

The moonlight upon his watch-dial showed one o'clock. The silence of the wilderness seemed to close round him impenetrably. But as he walked towards the post he thought he heard afar off the dull rattle of wheels among the rocks of the canon. When he arrived at the trader's store the sound had grown louder, and he paused out of mere wakefulness and curiosity until the phantom mail, for which he cared so little and had not yet even seen, should come. Soon the four little black heads were dancing along above the roadside chapparal, and the driver, his hand upon his mouth, was uttering hideous coyote-calls. Jehu seemed merry, for the mail was from the west, the worst was passed, and home and rest was only twenty miles away. That is a long distance upon which to congratulate one's self, the moody physician thought; but happiness is only a relative term. A strap was broken, and while the driver mended it and the sleepy clerk stood at the door, Peg inspected the wheels, the boot, and cautiously, the heels of the mules. Presently she seemed strangely attracted by something inside. She stood upon her hinder legs, and with her paws upon the broken window-frame, struggled, yelping, to climb up. This amazed the doctor, and he also drew near. Then a feminine voice was heard inside, and a white hand appeared in the moonlight, which the dog devotedly licked. Then the door was flung open and a woman's face appeared, and before Peg could effect an entrance her shaggy neck was clasped in feminine arms and audible kisses rained upon her hairy face. " Oh, you dear old dog! where *did* you come from?" were the words the doctor thought he heard. He certainly thought it a strange proceeding too, as who would not? He went to the window and said, " Peg—old girl;" and Peg thumped her large tail upon the bottom of the coach, and turned from one to the other and panted, and seemed agonized between two great happinesses.

Then the following conversation occurred, interrupted by little gasps and swallowings:

"Doctor—Daniels! who—who— My goodness! [evidently recovering] *is* it you?"

"Madge — Maggie! [huskily, and leaning very far forward] where *have* you been?"

"*Everywhere*, Sir, [entirely recovered,] to California last.',

" Well, but where—how?"

" This is what I have to say to you, Ed"—and the woman's voice grew strong in its tone of injury and right—" that no matter how you came here, or where from, you must go with me here and now, or I shall just get out and stay here, as I've a right to do I'm sure. And then I've been so far, and am *so* tired, and,—and,—I think I must be dreaming after all," and then this Amazon broke down and sobbed.

The doctor never looked so earnest at the bedside of a dying man as he did at this moment. He took off his hat solemnly, and the cool wind played with his damp locks. With his heart and his happiness there in the shabby coach, he stood fighting his pride outside. Then a hand reached forth and touched his shoulder, and a voice said, "I'm very sorry, Ed;" and immediately Doctor Edward Daniels turned resolutely and climbed into the coach. Those four words decided the question. He left everything behind, caring nothing for the morning astonishment of his late associates; for the criticisms of his enemies or the regrets of his friends. In this strange meeting all the past was forgotten, and all the future glowed with a new life, for he had again taken by the hand a love which had been wilful, capricious and exacting, but which, coming to him again, he eagerly grasped with all its forgiven sins. Jehu had been listening and chuckling to himself. "I rec'n she's got him," he said; and the noisy machine rattled away up the hill in the moonlight, with Doctor Daniels and his wife Margaret as passengers, and the dumb friend who had brought them together after years of estrangement, regret and search, lying at their feet. "I'm sure it's all very curious," remarked the now thoroughly awakened lady an hour afterwards; "but her name is *not* Peg at all. And Ed,—I'd like to see any of those Watkins girls wearing *my* dresses."

CAPTAIN JINKS.

IT is necessary in the beginning to caution the reader against misapprehension. This chapter does not contemplate the discussion of the merits or peculiarities of that gem in the repertory of the *opera bouffe*, which has some time since been sung and acted to its death. But there is a deal of truth told in broad burlesque; if it makes a palpable impression upon the public there must always be truth in the foundation. The genius, whoever he may be, who wrote " Captain Jinks" had a truthful portrait in his mind when he concocted the atrocious jingle and called it a song. Very few of those who have heard it, and still fewer of those who have sung it, ever saw anything in it beyond a little fun, and an opportunity for some stalwart actress, with startling physical development and a wonderful yellow wig, to mince before the footlights and display her misconception of him who, more than even Dundreary, is the ideal of gentlemanly snobbery.

As hinted, Captain Jinks is not entirely a myth, but there have been better conceptions of the professional soldier in more lasting literature. Thackeray must have watched him as he sauntered down the street and gone home and made a character of him. Dickens had an inkling of what was the matter with him, though he leaned rather toward the more devoted and more constantly employed naval officer.

It is more than probable that that large class of men who are idle, careless, dressy, free-and-easy and saucy, in time of peace, and brave, enduring, self-sacrificing and active in time of war, are much the same the world over. There has ever been among mankind a weakness for the sound of the drum, the rustle of a banner that represented a common cause, whatever that cause might be; the glint of bullion and the measured tread of battalions, and the touch of that slender, glittering thing which in all time has stood for justice, honor, and not unfrequently for that right which, with the change of its initial letter, means a very different thing. It is this common passion which makes the varied uniforms of the world cover hearts very nearly alike in what they love and hate.

But there is one of whom we desire to speak, who of all the soldiers of the world, is least known on fashionable streets and is most seldom seen at select parties and in the choice seats at the opera. With civilization and its pleasures and occupations he has little to do. There are no gay seasons and long leaves for him. Of all the homes along the far border of a growing republic his home is farthest away and most isolated. He is the soldier of a country which has the brightest and newest banner of all, whose silken folds represent to him all there is of abstract devotion and love; a country which in its last struggle raised and sent to the field the most intelligent, enduring, undaunted and brilliant armies the world probably ever saw; a country which in a single year, in the midst of divided sentiment, could rouse in her sons all the traditional courage, skill, valor and patriotism which lurks in the hearts of a long peaceful but a fighting and a glory-loving race. But in the end they sank again into the office, the shop and the furrow as mysteriously as sank the targe and plaid of the followers of Roderic Dhu upon the mountain-side, and he, the last remainder of a host, thinks, not without cause, that his cold-shouldered country has almost forgotten him.

Under all these disadvantages the United States army officer claims intimate kinship with his brethren of the buttons the world over. There are none who wear with more jauntiness a modest blue coat and the very tightest and nattiest of trowsers and boots, or whose gay little caps are more perilously perched upon the forward right-hand corner of an ambrosial head. In the matter of mustaches he excells the German, and in vivacity of movement he is beyond the Frenchman. He is a rattling shot at billiards and very cool and silent at whist. He has an eye for the points of horses and really and truly adores womankind with a devotion and strength which cavils at nothing they may do, say or think, and which, had he no other virtue, would keep him forever in the great brotherhood of gentlemen. He is isolated and utterly cut off from that world which is all there is to most of us, and his world comprises only arms, orders and duty.

But here in mountain fastnesses and the utter and dreary isolation of the wilderness, you strangely come upon the only genuine chivalry extant in American life. I may be taken to task for this wholesale statement, for the over-busy, nervous, money-getting citizens of this great republic claim all qualities as their own. Therefore I will explain. Chivalry in its essence means not a careless, but a very careful regard for the opinions, feelings and personal comfort of others, but more especially women. Besides that it means entire but polite candor, and no tricks in trade or anything else. It means that the affairs of life are conducted "on honor." Captain Jinks in the wilderness practises this and has practised it for so long that while staid and respectable citizens might smile contemptuously at his punctiliousness, they, together with their wives and daughters, would find him a most pleasant companion, and do well to try and find time to imitate some of his utterly foolish airs.

Do the gentlemen who sit a-row at attractive loitering places on our public streets in summer afternoons, rise up *en masse* when one poor little woman passes by? And if they do not and are excused for that, are they ever carefully watching lest some masculine phrase should reach her ear, or the cigar smoke should blow in her face? Is a woman's request a binding law if it be a possible thing? Most of these questions must be answered in the negative. Very often the American gentleman upon the street accosts his female friend with his hat over his eyes, his hands in his pockets and with a lazy politeness which indicates that he would fain have her think he was just as good as she. The knot of well-dressed vagabonds who own the adjoining houses and stand in the middle of the walk, say very distinctly to every woman who has the courage to pass through them: "home and to the dishes, my dear; the street was made for men."

We may go further and leave out women and inquire how Captain Jinks excels us. He takes off his hat in his own office or room and does likewise when he comes into yours. He expects to be offered a seat, and if you let him stand he leaves as quickly as possible and don't come back any more. He don't back-bite and insinuate, and you can't tell upon your first acquaintance with him what and who he likes and hates. Such things with him lead to very rapid settlements of difficulties, and Jinks is therefore, as we should all be, careful. There is no need of any action for slander there, for words and opinions are supposed to be valuable and are cautiously used. He will lend or give you anything you ask, but you must not ask. There are other things he will do upon proper invitation not so much to his credit. A little sip of something from a mahogany case is seldom offered at the wrong time o'day. A little shuffling of a clean deck and an unimportant transfer of green currency is generally agreeable when he isn't busy, and he never is. Jinks is frivolous, over-polite, *nonchalant*, and carries a very high nose, but he will fight. An intimation that he wouldn't would hasten matters very fast in that direction. And the ugliest antagonist in the world, is this same tender-handed fop, because it is in his line of business. He stands in the same relation to the rest of mankind in this respect that the terrier does to dogs; he spends no time in considering the size of his antagonist. But the science of projectiles is his *forte*. Only of late years has the *duello* came to be looked upon as wrong and foolish by the best class of army officers. Elderly gentlemen, long since retired to office chairs, have recollections of that sort which they sometimes mention, and in these instances death is always bargained for, yet seldom achieved.

Captain Jinks is a strictly professional man, and after some years of military life, knows more of his specialty than he is generally given credit for. There is a common impression that to own a commission signed by the President and wear a blue coat is to be a soldier. But the traditional routine, the customs, the business and the accurate drill, require years in their mastery. The army is partially governed by an unwritten code, which has as much binding force as the common law. You would not suspect that Jinks was ever a business man, yet the great system of accountability for public property requires something very little short of business talent for its proper comprehension. It is the most endless and intricate bundle of tape imaginable to the beginner, but clear and accurate to the practised quartermaster. The government is a hard creditor, and will stop Jinks' pay for an old padlock, ten years after the loss occurred, if things come to the worst. He is responsible for all the houses, and scattered odds and ends, and fuel and forage of a post as large as a respectable village; the residence of hundreds of people. Wagons, caisons, mules, warehouses, shops, tools and material are all on his "papers," and must be cared for and counted and kept straight. Every company commander must be a business man, and has a running account with a hundred men. Military efficiency means money, and the first qualification of an army officer of any grade or station is economy and good judgment in the care of property and the spending of money. That diligence, care and accuracy, to say nothing of honesty, are as much required here as in private business, the fact only need be mentioned, that many gentlemen who were not such extraordinary quartermasters and commissaries, have since shown themselves to be bankers, brokers, etc., of tolerable efficiency.

Nor is this all. Like an editor, Jinks must have a very varied and extensive fund of information. He is alike an autocrat and a justice of the peace. He is the head and leader of a hundred careless, and often ignorant, childish or vicious men. He learns, during his intercourse with them, to intimately know each one, though at a distance. He is often called upon to exercise the functions of priest, physician and executor to the same man. He must know how to exercise at once kindness and firmness, and with unlimited power, to command the fullest respect and some degree of love. If there is a foible, a weakness, a want of courage or capacity on the part of their commander, be sure the ranks will find it out.

Jinks and his companions have made some of the most daring and careful explorations of modern times. They traversed the mountain by-ways of the far west more than a score of years ago, and mapped and described the great plains long before railways and immigration were thought of. They did all this learnedly and skilfully and without any reward. There is today a more accurate knowledge of the climates, characteristics, geography and natural history of the world west of the Missouri in the United States army than there is among all the *savans*.

Perhaps, finally, it may not be uninteresting to know how Captain Jinks lives. The reign of monotony and silence hedges him in. Nowhere, within reaching distance, are any of those things which make life pleasant. He has but to go a little distance from the flag-staff to be utterly alone. Yet so far as his little acre of actual occupancy goes, he has transformed the wilderness. Here is a quadrangular space, as neatly kept as a parlor floor; in the center floats always the sheeny representative of that for which the soldier lives. On every hand are the oddly-shaped houses, sometimes handsome and costly, often only log cabins or adobes. But you will find nothing like squalor within. There is comfort and neatness always, and not unfrequently elegance and a slight suggestion of luxury. As a rule, Jinks and his wife care little for the house itself so that the furnishing reaches the proper standard of comfort and taste. There are books, music, curtains, carpets, a very well-furnished table and a very fair display of china and silver. Jinks is something of an epicure, and often in his far home dines upon dainties which an alderman could not procure. He saves himself from an hour of inanity every afternoon by thinking what he will have for dinner, and then goes and asks every unengaged person he can find to come and help him eat it. You wonder as you watch this hospitable soldier in his meanderings where he finds the spice of content. In these houses are elegant and well-dressed women, though peradventure their gowns may not be strictly in the fashion and their social gossip not of the latest sensation.

Around this nucleus cluster the thousand surroundings and belongings of civilization. Horses neigh in populous stables, and mules bray in the corral. The sound of the hammer and file are heard, and the wood-yard and warehouse are in busy operation. There is the trader's store, an immensely attractive spot, which may be called the club-room of the border. There the loafing instinct which Jinks has in common with the rest of mankind, is gratified by the clatter of ivory balls and the aroma of tobacco.

These are the means by which he keeps up his connection with and his interest in the world which, with all its enjoyable things he has almost forgotten. There is no danger that he will degenerate. The discipline of his daily life would keep him from that. His military ceremonies are performed in full dress, and midnight on the lonely guard-beat, sees the inopportune pomp of "grand-rounds," as ceremoniously done as though in view of the commander-in-chief.

But do and say what we will, Captain Jinks *will*

swagger, will persist in regarding all professions below par in comparison with his, and will so persist in carrying an air of careless superiority with him wherever he goes, that the more sombre-clad and quiet portion of mankind must necessarily dislike him. But we must be allowed to remark that he would be a poor soldier, if he was not guilty of these things. It is only when he is placed among civilians that they are noticeable, and they are the direct result of a professional training, of which a man cannot be expected to divest himself as he puts off a garment. He is no soldier who is not proud of his uniform, and in nine cases in ten you will find the American soldier an honest man and in its strictest sense, a gentleman. His life in peace is one long preparation for that hour of his country's need when he shall lead the blue line he has so often drilled, up to the battery, and follow the starry emblem he has so often gathered in his arms as it came down at the sunset gun, into the jaws of death. Every year he endures hardships at the frontier camp-fire, of which he shows no sign as you see him passing by. We cannot blame him if he be a little proud of the slender blade which, after all, is not his but his country's. Let us not be mistaken in our Captain Jinks. Of such as he,—just such foppish, careless fellows,—have ere now grown great generals, lamented heroes, statesmen and presidents. Useless ornament though he may be, and reminder of the strength of monarchies rather than of peaceful democracies, time has been that a few more available Jinkses would have saved our country many a life and many a million of treasure, when, in impending peril, we scarce knew the equipment of a camp or the duties of a picket-guard.

JORNADA DEL MUERTO.

ONE evening about sunset, in the year 1869, the vehicle which is by courtesy called a coach, drawn by four little mules, with its driver and expressman, and four passengers inside, started out of Peraja on the southward journey, which few who have made it will forget, and which afterwards seems a strange adventure, undertaken by night, and for some purpose which was itself a dream.

Peraja is, as the name indicates, the very dogsburg of a land of squalid towns. It is as though it had been gently shaken in a blanket, and indiscriminately dropped in the midst of a few acres of sand. Sand is there an element. It blows through every chink and cranny, and lies ankle-deep in the street. It pervades all that is eaten and drunk and breathed, and lies in winrows and heaps. But this is all in accordance with the Mexican idea, for a few hundred yards away the ground is grass-grown and hard, and that which stands in the changing sand by chance might easily have been placed on solid earth on purpose. Worse than all, it stands at the hither end of that ninety miles of treeless, waterless wilderness, which to many has been in fact all that the poetic name implies: *jornada del muerto*—" the journey of death."

Of the four passengers, one was an acting medical officer in the army; one was a trader; one a man who was anything and had no characteristics; and the fourth, a large man in middle life, who sat with his back to the front and his long limbs thrown across the middle seat, was as evidently a genuine son of the frontier as though the fact had been placarded upon him. His magnificent beard was plentifully sprinkled with gray, and the soles of his great boots, upright before his audience, seemed as though they might serve for tombstones, if he should chance to follow an old-time fashion of his kind and be buried in them. His slouch hat was pulled low over a pair of gray eyes and a kindly, honest face, and he held the Winchester gun across his knee with that careless yet constant grasp which is one of the small signs betokening a man used to danger, and accustomed to the vigilance which in those regions becomes a habit.

The gold and purple and amber faded, and the far snow grew pink and gray, then whiter than before in the starlight, and soon there was nothing of earth in the scene save the tall cactuses that took fantastic shapes as they nodded in the light of the horizon, and the vague and misty undulations of a wilderness which, clothed in night and silence, seemed a part of some other and unreal world.

Four women together, strange to each other, and without a counterpoise of masculinity, would either keep silence or politely disagree. But men do not; and by this time each one had given his fellows some idea of who he was, where he was born, and what he liked best of men, horses, climates and cookery. Not specifically and in order, but as men tell such things. Such revelations come first naturally. Then comes a little modest bragging on the part of each, and he who goes too far in that is straightway snubbed into snappishness or docility, either of which mental conditions answers the purpose equally well. After this comes silence, yawning, and finally sleep. Only part of this program could be carried out here. Sociability was a necessity, for if four men sleep on the *Jornada* they may never wake again. No man listens to his neighbor's story or becomes absorbed in his own so intently that his ear is not also alert for the far-away galloping or the sudden shout which betokens the Apache.

The intense desire for something outside one's own thoughts is as universal as humanity. To this end is all the immense literature which is born in a night and dies in the morning. For the gratification of an appetite which is insatiable, are the remotest corners of the earth ransacked, and all that is done and suffered in all climes and races condensed into paragraphs and laid even at the day-laborer's door. But where this is impossible and unknown, its place is taken by an art the oldest and most graceful in the world—the art of story-telling. To the borderer, the ability to wander pleasantly through the past of his life, to cause his limited audience to see his situations as plainly as he remembers them, and to call out the laugh or curse which is his applause and reward, is considered a matter of course. The silent man has few friends. But no man is asked formally or in turn to tell a story. He begins as soon as he can get an audience by cutting in on his neighbor's fast-waning discourse, and he continues through a running fire of comments, jokes and minor adventures. This, with the addition of some show of form, is the vaunted Indian oratory. It is the common characteristic of wild humanity everywhere, and is simplest and most attractive where form is absent, and humor and pathos lack egotism and consciousness.

For the most part the large man was silent. His companions were none of them of the class to which he was accustomed as auditors. The trader told of circumstances which had transpired in a country neighborhood in some eastern State, and duly mentioned the names and relationships of all his characters. The medical man told of college adventures and flirtations, and touched a little upon science. The man who was nothing, and had no character, sat silent, only occasionally throwing in an interjection or exclamation of wonder. This made him popular with the doctor and the trader.

Finally that waning, red morning-moon, which is but the ghost of brightness, and which seems to steal around the verge of the universe at late hours to avoid being seen, rose slowly above the horizon and added a little light. The dreary undulations of the landscape grew more distinct. Thirty miles of the journey lay behind, and the lonely backward track, and the still lonelier yet to come, oppressed the party with that vague uneasiness which some of them had never felt before.

But now a change seemed to have come over the frontiersman. As his companions grew silent he grew active. He peered curiously out upon the road, and seemed intent upon the outlines of the hills. He arose and stood with his foot upon the step, and looked ahead and behind and close beside the track. He excited the curiosity of his companions, who long since had set him down as stupid, and they improved the opportunity presented for new amusement.

"Ever been here before?" said the doctor.

"You bet!"

"Oh," said the trader, "*lived* here?"

"I rec'n I spent ten thousand dollars not a mile from this 'ere spot."

"Looking for it?"

The big man bent his huge figure beneath the curtains

and lounged back into his seat, drew a long breath, pushed back his hat and remarked :

"I'll tell you all about it."

"Go ahead," said the doctor.

"I've heerd you boys talk for about six hours. Now I'm goin' to talk some myself; but I would n't, unless this 'ere place did n't remind me of it. Fust of all, there aint nothin'—nary thing—in grit an' pluck an' sense, and all that. There 's nothin' but luck—jest luck.

"I come out from Missoury to Californy in '49. They was flush times then, and money was as plenty as water, and plentier. But a man could n't make nothin', and after two year I had n't much more money than I've got now, which the same aint much. But while I stayed there I spent more, had more fun and more fights, and cared less, than any man in Californy. And then, as was nat'ral in sich cases, things begun to go bad with me, and times to git close, and in '54 I come down through Arizony and them parts. In Tucson, in two weeks, I win ten thousand dollars at poker—luck. Then I jest stopped short. I laid low for about four days 'tell I got a chance, and then come on into this yer infernal country with my money. I had a mind to stop gamblin' and try an' git a livin' like some men I've *heerd* of—honestly. I knowed a man's luck did n't giner'ly do him a good turn more 'n once, and I concluded to go back on it in time. I got down here to Cruces, and some fellers pusuaded me to come out here into this infernal *hornado* and dig fur water. A passel of us come out here and found a swale——" Here the speaker crowded out again, and for some minutes was engaged in looking intently for some feature in the landscape.

"I thought I seed the place," said he, as he resumed his seat.

"Where you left the money?" said the doctor.

"This thing I'm a tellin' aint no joke to *me*," he quietly remarked presently. "Both of you fellers has said somethin' smart now, about the last pile I ever had,—or am like to have,—and the next smart thing I propose to say *myself*. As I was sayin', we found a swale where it looked damp. Me an' my party, we dug an' dug. There aint no man knows any better 'n me how to make a hole in the ground. I larned that in Californy. But we didn't find no water. Afore we was through, we dug all over this cussed desert, and finally I swallered the fact that I had n't no more money."

"Is that so?" chirped the medical man.

"Wait till I tell you. D—n it, it riles me to think of it," thundered the speaker. "*That* wan't the wust of it. Afore that missable diggin' I had gone and—and married. She *wus* the pootiest thing in Mexico. I tell you I aint *never* seed no woman to suit me sence, and she's—gentle*men*,—she's been dead fourteen year, and that's the wust luck I *ever* had."

The story-teller cleared his throat and went on: "Well, after that I went down to the settlements ag'in, and after that the Guv'ment sent some people here, and *they* dug and bored all over the country, and spent thousands of dollars, and didn't find no water. The whole thing looked like a bad job, and folks made up their minds to go without water. Plenty of 'em didn't. This 'ere road hes been the end o' many a mule, to say nothin' of other people. And now what do you think they tell me in Santa Fe? Why, they say a man named Tom suthin', I forgit what; a feller that *never* had no luck, a kind of animile which was wuthless when sober and mean when drunk, come out here last summer and commenced a diggin', *and struck water in sixty foot.* He has a ranch now, and a Guv'ment contract, and a wife and babies. Congress giv him all the land in sight, and he's sober, and makes money. Aint *that* luck?"

The speaker seemed irritable, and brought down his great fist with a thump upon the seat beside him.

"Why yes," said the doctor, "everybody knows that. We'll reach the place about five o'clock. I wish *I* was there now."

Silent men sometimes grow preternaturally communicative, and the speaker continued: "And do you know what I come down here for? Don't? Well I'll tell you. 'Cause I'm a fool. There's people that visits graveyards and things where thur friends is. I'm goin' back, now, to see if I kin find *my* cimetry. I've tried everything else since I was there last, and sometimes I've concluded I'd nigh about forgot it. 'Pears to me I'm gittin' old now, and the hankerin' comes stronger. I don't know where the grave is I'm a huntin.' P'raps there ain't none; but I want to see the place where,— ahem—I lost my woman I hadn't had a year."

The strong man seemed to be growing strangely weak. He breathed hard, and nervously fanned himself with his hat. Then he sat for a few minutes looking dreamily out, and in the midst of his reverie, muttered disconnected anathemas upon the Apaches. After a while he continued:

"You see I went back to the settlements from here, and jined a party goin' back to Californy. I tuk what little I had left, and owned one team out'n the twenty-eight which was in the train,—me an' my wife. I wan't broke any *then*. I was big an' strong, and didn't mind my luck much it seemed like. We got a fair start airly in September, and was a goin' back by way of Arizony of course. There's a place about a hundred mile from here on t'other trail, called—somebody's Canon,—the wust place fur Injuns in the world. We camped at a spring at this eend all night, and airly in the mornin' started through. When we got about two-thirds of the way through, at a suddint turn in the road, the first team come chuck up agin a barricade o' rocks, an' a *swarm* of 'Paches come down on us from all sides. We'd passed a pass'l o' soldiers on the road, but of course, as luck'd have it, they wan't there. That 'ere, gentlemen, was the worst massacre I've ever knowed of. Ther wan't *no* help, an' they jest had the jump on us. I 'member at the first, seein' some of the wimmin' jump out 'n the wagons and run screamin' down among the *chapparal*, tryin' to hide. I was up in the lead, an' started back to where my outfit was, fust thing. I never got there. Suthin' or somebody struck me over the head from behind."

Here the speaker took off his hat, and leaning forward, bade his auditors place their fingers upon a deep and ugly scar upon his head.

"I fell down an' I rec'lect gittin' up ag'in and runnin' on and on. It seemed as though I never got where I wanted to, an' I turned dizzy, an' commenced a gittin' blind. But I kep' a goin' till all of a suddint I forgot everything. When I come to my senses it must 'a been a week afterwards. *I* never knowed, but it was on a narrer bed in a hospital, at a camp that's 'bolished now, fifty mile west of that ar' Canon. You see them soldiers come along after us,—too late. I allus heerd that the last livin' soul was killed. But they found me *somewhar*, an' toted me along as them fellers knows how to do. One day I kinder woke up, layin' on a narrer bed in a 'dobe house, an' a big bearded feller in a uniform was a holdin' of my wrist, and lookin' down at me, an' smilin' like he was nigh tickled to death. I tell you,"—with a glance at the medical man, "he *wus* a doctor. I crawled roun' that place till I was strong agin' and kep' thinkin' it all over. I concluded I was the only man left. I was riled, an' I listed in them Second Dragoons, a purpose for to kill Injuns. I cared fur nothin' else then, an' I served out five years 'listment. Then I went back to Californy. But since then I aint had no luck. I aint done no good for years. It's been months now sence I've thort of anything but that day in the canon. I tell ye, sometimes I kinder think may be my wife and some of them wimmen got away! 'Taint so. I *know* 'taint so, an' its no use to speckerlate. What do I care *now?* She was a *pooty* thing, an' sly, an' smart. But what makes me think of her is beyand *that*. You see she was ailin a little,—wa'nt very well, and ef she'd a lived a week longer "—

He did not finish the sentence, and leaning forward placed his great hands over his face and sat silent. After a while he resumed:

"Gentlemen, 't would n't be any use fur you to tell me I'm a fool. I've been a thinkin' of this for fourteen year, and now it's got to be I aint good fur nothin' else. Other men has their youngsters an' never thinks of it, but I can 't hear a baby cry—which I hain't often—'thout gittin' kind o' weak. But there 's one thing I *kin* do. I'm goin' to find that place in the canon. I 've as good a right to visit *my* family cimetry as any man livin'—" and the speaker grew excited as he thus combated the idea of being foolish in the premises; but he tremulously added: "I 'd give all that ten thousand, and all the water there is on the *hornado*, if I cud *see*, jest once, that baby that never was born."

None of the men he had spoken to were fools, but all had been mistaken in their conception of the frontiersman. He was now invested with a new interest. So far as they knew he was the only survivor of one of the most fearful of all the Indian massacres of that country. They respected the story and the feelings of one to whom that day had been a brooding memory for so many years. The physician at least was a man of some learning, culture and delicacy of feeling. He divined the tender spot in this giant which his and his companion's raillery had touched, and now felt the peculiar leaning toward him which all his cloth experience in connection with what bids fair to be "a special case."

"See here, my friend," said he, "who told you that your—ah, your wife, was actually killed? I would 'nt raise your hopes, you know; but then there 's no telling about such things unless you actually *know*. *You* are alive, you see, and—ah, well, you can't 'most always tell." He ended with a laugh. He thought he would say something comforting, and had broken down and ended with a slang expression. Such are ever your male comforters. Presently he continued: "Now you see, the chances are, if things were as you state, that—ah, in view of the excitement and fight, you know, the little fellow would be born then and there, and—ah, if the mother was strong, you know, why you may yet see the ch—"

He suddenly stopped, for the frontiersman was leaning forward in his seat, and with quick breath drinking in every word. "My God!" he said, "*do* you think so? Air you in *yearnest?* Nobody told me she was dead,— and *everybody*. But she is—she is, and if she was n't, it would n't know *me*."

"It! Who?" said the medical man.

"*The baby!*"

The short summer night began to fade, and that rare first glimpse of sunlight upon mountain snow, which more than anything in nature bears the similitude of a kiss, began to appear. The tired beasts seemed to take new life, and pushed eagerly on. Far in the distance could be dimly heard the first crowing of the cocks, the bleating of goats, and the cry of asses, while the thin blue breakfast-smoke could be seen curling from the chimney of the little adobe castle, which was the "lucky" man's ranche.

The proprietor was a sandy-haired fellow, half Yankee, half Irishman. All the frontiersmen had heard of him was true. He *had* a wife and babies, and a Government contract, and it was his first luck. He was happy, and he ushered the four travellers into the house as though he had known them for years. He had a protege, the child of a Mexican servant, whom he considered one of the attractions of his place, and of whom he was wonderfully proud. When she came into the room at these early breakfasts, he always dilated upon the girl and her peculiar history. The facts warranted him. She was a creature of fourteen, who looked twenty. She had an enormous quantity of that glorious red hair which s crimson in the sunshine, and eyes which were big and black. She was round and lithe and graceful, and was, in short, a rare specimen of the being which sometimes springs from the healthful admixture of two races.

"Do you see that garl, gentlemen?" says he. "That's the handsomest little thing in Mexico, and differs from thim all, in her birthplace and h r nursin'. Sure her mother's me cook, and nothin' to m , and I've plenty of me own, but they was born in a h\ se." And with that he hurried away to attend to some necessary things, intending by all means to hasten back and finish his proud tale.

The four travellers sat and watched with some eagerness the preparations for breakfast. From time to time entered the girl and her mother, busied with household affairs. The latter seemed an almost middle-aged Spanish woman of the better kind, care-worn and wrinkled as all her class are when youth fades. She was accustomed to strangers and did not notice that the huge frontiersman had regarded her from her first entrance with a kind of dreamy stare. The *frijoles* and the *chile—con—carne* had occupied her attention, and she almost screamed when the big man rose up in her way, his gray eyes glittering and his lips white, and faintly spoke a word in Spanish,—so faintly that none understood.

She did not let fall the brown dish she held in her hand; she was ignorant of nerves and sensations: but she placed it upon the table and looked steadily at him. Her face blanched with fear and horror. As slow recognition dawned upon her, she sank down upon the floor and turned away her head, muttering " *O caro Jesus,—retroceder de la muerte!*

" But I am n't returned from the dead," said he. "I'm Bob,—Big Bob. W'y now look here,—say! don't go away. I'm dr'nk, or crazy, or dreamin,' or else you are,—*my wife!*

She arose while he spoke, and the look of terror changed to one of consternation and anxiety. " Oh go away," she said in her lisping English, " it is so long, so long; since the other husband—*mucho muchacha;*" and she passed backward through the door, her face full of a great apprehension. What wonder? Dead husbands are not wanted to come back again and interrupt the social relations which come about through their deaths. This Spanish woman had a second living husband, even then in the dooryard, and acted as many of you would in a situation so strange and so nearly impossible.

Then the proprietor returned and proceeded to finish his remarks. "I was about to remark to ye, gentlemin, about this garl, that her mother was one of the only two persons who come out alive from the massacre in the canon a dozen years ago. This garl—come 'ere Chuck—was born there among the *chaparral*, where her mother and t' other woman hid at the first of the scare, and she lived and growed, and its a beauty, sure."

The frontiersman listened as one who dreams. His eyes rested softly and lovingly upon the child, who knew and cared as little for *him* as though he were indeed dead in the canon. "*Chicquita,*" said he as he advanced toward her and held out his hand, "do ye know who I am? Yer mother does. W'y now come!—can't ye?" His fond and confident look changed to one almost of agony as the girl ran from him with a wondering look, and took refuge beside the proprietor.

"Look here Mister," said the Irishman, "I don't know *you*, but you must be a fool. What are ye a skeerin' of this one for? Now stop yer foolin' and eat yer breakfast if ye want to, and if not, be done wid yer nonsense in me house."

"She's my own little one," thundered the other. "I'm her *father!* Go call her mother to tell ye—and mind yer jaw or I'll—" Then the woman, with red eyes, and a face in which a strange contest was visible, again entered the room.

"No, Senor," said she. "I not know you—go." And she sank into a corner, and covered her face and rocked to and fro.

The Irishman seemed reassured. Therefore he advanced upon his antagonist. "Who are you?" he said. "The man you claim to be is dead long ago. He was dead when this garl was born. You can't play no sich stuff as that. 'Taint none of this one ye'll git now. She won't look at you. Chuck, who is this felley anyhow?"

The spoiled beauty looked disdainfully toward the frontiersman, contemplated him for a moment, and broke into a careless laugh.

The victim of all this sunk into a seat like one stricken. The actions of the child were natural, and the instinctive recognition of relationships is but a fable. The actions of the mother were, perhaps, equally so. She had said, "so long—so long," and what she meant by it was true. The broken-hearted man, denied by his wife, derided by his child,—of whose possible existence he had vaguely dreamed for so many years—and insulted and defied by an uninterested but officious stranger, crept away and hid himself in the coach, and was there when it drove out of the yard on its onward journey.

The remaining fifty miles were travelled in the glow and cheerfulness of day, but the party was now a quiet and constrained one. The physician and the trader conversed apart, in instinctive deference to the mood of their companion, who sat in his old seat, pale, haggard, and seemingly crushed by that century of suffering which to some in this life is concentrated into a single hour. Years seemed added to his age.

The conversation between the two gentlemen grew more earnest and confidential, and finally, as by agreement, the physician left his seat, and placed himself beside the frontiersman. The touch of the kind man's hand,—the hand of a physician with a heart,—was almost a caress, as he said, "Now my friend, Wiggins and I have been talking about this,—ah, this trouble of yours. If you need any help of any kind, we want to know it. We also want to say we are sorry for anything we said last night, which was,—ah, not agreeable you know. I am stationed at Selden. We'll be there this evening you know, and I think, perhaps,—ah, that you had better stay awhile with me."

When at last the post was reached, it seemed with difficulty that the stranger walked to the doctor's quarters. As the days passed on, he failed to appear. The collossal strength became childish weakness. Every sign of age had smitten him. But the pillow on which the gray head lay was softer than any he had ever felt before. The great beard which streamed over the coverlet, and grew whiter every day, seemed a fit setting for the strong features, changing hourly now into more perfect peace.

The words and the scene which had wrecked the last hope of this man's life had made no change in the routine at the ranche. The woman kept her secret. Her husband never heard or dreamed of the situation; and the careless girl only remembered as an incident the old man's admiration.

I would that that mother and daughter could have been near, that autumn afternoon, when the big emaciated hand was held by the last friend he ever had, and could have heard, when he said: "Good-bye. I'm glad to go. I couldn't help it. I never had no luck. It's all right now."

And for the last time,—lonelier now than before, but with no fear, nor danger nor thirst,—the frontiersman started out upon *jornada del muerto*.

www.ingramcontent.com/pod-product-compliance
Lightning Source LLC
Chambersburg PA
CBHW021355230426
43666CB00006B/528